# KEEP TURNING RIGHT

## YOU'LL GET THERE EVENTUALLY

# RICK DAPP

SUNBURY
P R E S S

Mechanicsburg, PA  USA

Published by Sunbury Press, Inc.
50 West Main Street
Mechanicsburg, Pennsylvania 17055

SUNBURY
PRESS

**www.sunburypress.com**

For information about special discounts for bulk purchases, please contact Sunbury Press Orders Dept. at (855) 338-8359 or orders@sunburypress.com.

To request one of our authors for speaking engagements or book signings, please contact Sunbury Press Publicity Dept. at publicity@sunburypress.com.

ISBN: 978-1-62006-610-2 (Trade Paperback)
ISBN: 978-1-62006-611-9 (Mobipocket)

Library of Congress Control Number: 2015947556

FIRST SUNBURY PRESS EDITION: July 2015

*Product of the United States of America*
0 1 1 2 3 5 8 13 21 34 55

Set in Bookman Old Style
Designed by Crystal Devine
Cover by Amber Rendon
Edited by Janice Rhayem

*Continue the Enlightenment!*

For Tris

# CONTENTS

# PREFACE

Prefaces are often ignored portions of books, in which authors attempt to enlighten the reader regarding the pages to follow, and this is no exception. It is valuable only in the sense that it provides an explanation of the title and possibly a little of the content.

It was an experience with my dad that provided the title for this book. Once, when I was hopelessly lost in downtown Ann Arbor, Michigan, (a city of seemingly all one-way streets) I called him from a pay phone and expressed my frustration at ever finding my way out of my predicament. His reply was, "Keep turning right, you'll get there eventually." Those words stayed with me and, despite a variety of wrong turns in life, I always fell back upon the simple logic of his statement.

The book is not intended as a solution to the problem of unemployment, as many "how-to" books profess, but is, rather, a "how-not-to" volume from someone who has lived the experience.

# 1.

# WHAT HAPPENS

The last thing I expected in life was to become suddenly unemployed. Not that unemployment is extraordinary, it just didn't occur to me that it might happen to *me*, a (and I hate to use this term) "middle-aged" baby boomer. We have all followed those news stories about men in their fifties who worked for corporations and found themselves out on the street with few prospects for the future; it's just that I never envisioned myself joining them at age forty-seven.

After sixteen years working for a Fortune 200 electronics manufacturer in positions ranging from technical writer to marketing, I went to work one morning, a Thursday as a matter of fact (can you imagine letting someone go on a *Thursday*?), and the woman for whom I worked for said, "Can I talk to you for a few minutes?" This in itself may seem pretty innocuous to the average reader. But when you consider that the longest conversation I think I had with this person in the three months I reported to her consisted of brief greetings in the hallway, a sentence of nine words was unnervingly unprecedented.

Then came a quick trip to a conference room and some truly heartfelt phrases like "industry downturn" and "Asian crisis," followed by a walk downstairs to see the human resources representative (who informed me that she was probably going to be laid off after she finished processing everyone on *her* list). This left me standing outside the building with no card key and no job. The echoes of my manager's final comment ("If there's *anything* that I can do, please don't hesitate to call.") followed me and my cardboard box of desk items across the parking lot to my car.

I was suddenly unemployed. Completely.

# 2.

# WHAT TO EXPECT

The first day of unemployment is one of wonder and anticipation, kind of like taking the first day of a vacation from reality. After walking my son to the school bus and kissing my wife good-bye on her way to work (thank God for all those years of feeling slightly inadequate because she always had a better job than I did), I wandered around the house trying to think what I wanted to do first. I threw a load of laundry in the washing machine, cleaned up the kitchen, and started to watch the *Today Show* marveling at how very *free* I felt. This sense of elation lasted until lunchtime when I realized how much damn work there was to do around the house and who was going to have to do it with a household income that was suddenly cut in half.

At this point, signing up for unemployment compensation becomes a compelling factor in your life, and you make that fateful trip to the state unemployment office for your initial interview.

If you have never spent time at an unemployment office, you have missed one of life's truly bleak moments. I had heard tales of long lines and forms to be filled out and rejection at the window for filling out the shaded area incorrectly, but I wasn't prepared for the real experience. There were no lines (I took a number and sat in a reasonably comfortable plastic chair), the forms aren't *that* hard to figure out, and the woman at the counter waited patiently while I filled out the rest of the form. After doing the requisite paperwork, with number in hand, you take a seat and wait. And wait. And wait.

I've always considered patience one of my several virtues, but waiting for a claim interview at the unemployment office really challenged it. I looked around the waiting area and found no one who seemed even remotely interested in returning even a flash of whimsy in such a depressing place. Everyone stared at anything *but* the other human beings in the room, except for a group of three women who had an animated chat about a mutual supervisor at the manufacturing plant where they had worked prior to being laid off.

Finally, my number was called, and I went forward to meet with *my* claims representative. I approached him with trepidation, fully expecting to receive a thorough grilling regarding my career and personal aspirations. He glanced at my paperwork, asked me what my last full day of work was, initialed the form, handed it back to me, and told me what telephone number to call every two weeks to file my claim. He never made eye contact.

I was now officially a member of the tribe.

# 3.

# WHO YOU'LL MEET

Spending time at home allows you to interact with a segment of humanity that remains largely unknown to people who leave the house in the morning, work all day at a remote location, and return home in the evening. Did you ever wonder *who*, exactly, drops off those boxes from UPS or FedEx at your front door? Or how your fuel-oil tank magically becomes refilled on a regular basis? I know.

After spending years commuting and passing all of those gleaming brown trucks or the lumbering tankers that block half the street with a hose running from them into a house, I can now say that *actual* human beings are in charge here. It's interesting to talk to the person who drops off the package (although he, or she, is always in a hurry and making notations on a clipboard—usually electronic—during the conversation) and find out that they have a regular "route" and know the area as well as the postman. The fuel delivery guy (and I *will* say "guy" here, because I have never personally seen anyone other than a male driving one of these behemoths or pumping fuel from one—although, I am sure that somewhere there are women who do this) is generally more chatty than the UPS driver. I think that this is because they have more time to talk while waiting for the truck to pump the requisite amount into the tank.

Having the good fortune to live in the country means that we have a rural mail carrier, who *is* a woman. Her name is Helen, and she drives a Suzuki four-wheel drive (you know, the model that government said would roll over at the sign of the first stiff breeze) every day to deliver the mail. I think it's interesting that a federal employee uses a vehicle (it belongs to her) faithfully every day that was pretty well stiffed on television for being unsafe.

# 4.
## WHAT YOU'LL DO

You'll find yourself with time during the day to do things that you never would have dreamed of doing when you were employed full time ... like grocery shopping. I don't know why I thought grocery shopping would be easier during the day than it is during the evening or on weekends when *normal* people shop. I had visions of deserted aisles and cashiers restlessly waiting to run your purchases through the scanner. Instead, the grocery store was—if anything—busier than it seemed on a weekend with, get this, *retired people*! I had forgotten that retired people eat food, too! However, they are mostly friendlier than the crowd at the unemployment office.

Speaking of retired people, I did, fairly early in the experience, have a friend ask me what it was like to be unemployed, and, after thinking about it for a moment, told him that it was "like being retired without the money." He made some nice clucking noises (it was over the telephone), wished me well, and hung up.

That brings up another subject—friends. When you become suddenly unemployed, you find out just how many friends you have in the workplace. I found that I had five who actually called me (and continue to do so) to "see how I was doing" and offer some words of encouragement. The rest of those bastards who phoned me incessantly during the day and prevailed upon me constantly for data, advice, expedites, answers, products, rumors, catalogs, and more than my share of the load never called.

# 5.

# BLUE DAYS

It's inevitable that a suddenly unemployed person *will* have blue days. This is not to be confused with clinical depression, which is a series of deeply grim days that require medical attention. Blue days for the unemployed are the same as blue days for the employed, with the exception of having someone to share them. If you can remember, blue days at "work" were usually accompanied by statements to coworkers like, "Haven't you just about had the shits of this place?" Or, "I could have taught school, but nooooo ... I had to come *here*!" Or, "Jeez, I can't *believe* what a total moron that guy is!"

Blue days for the unemployed just don't have the rebound statements from another person to affirm your feelings.

Ten things to absolutely avoid on blue days:

1. Playing Bonnie Raitt's rendition of Randy Newman's song "Guilty."
2. Watching Bill Gates being interviewed.
3. Comparing your last pay stub with the unemployment check.

4. Shopping for anything.
5. Watching *any* talk show on TV, especially things like *The People's Court*. (Why on earth would you like to see other miserable people air *their* problems while you have *yours* to keep you company?)
6. Drinking anything stronger than coffee.
7. Calling or e-mailing former coworkers to "see what's happening."
8. Calling or e-mailing any personnel agency to "just touch base" and ask why you haven't heard from them lately.
9. Spending any time wondering why it was you, the hard working and loyal employee, who was "downsized" and not that guy down the hall who always seemed to have the solitaire game up on the screen of his PC.
10. Taking yourself too seriously.

Ten things to *do* on blue days:

1. Take a walk. It gets you out of the house and changes your perspective (those of you in high-crime areas may consider getting a treadmill and turning on the Nature Channel).
2. Do a load of laundry (yes, I know it's mindless, but it makes you feel as though you accomplished something).
3. Clean out a closet or your dresser (same effect as #2).
4. Take the unwanted clothing that you have removed from the closet or dresser to the Salvation Army or Goodwill and donate it (you'll feel better, and they give you a receipt for the items, which you can use as a tax deduction—if you ever have an income again).
5. Write notes to your favorite humans telling them that you love them.
6. Rearrange the furniture. (Your wife/husband/significant other will probably want you to return it to its original state, but you'll feel as though you made a *difference* in your world that day!)

7. Make a really elaborate dinner.
8. Change the message on your answering machine to reflect an upbeat personality (adding something like calypso music to the background might make it sound even better).
9. Install a bird feeder outside a window to see who shows up.
10. Play your favorite music real loud—unless that's Bonnie Raitt singing Randy Newman's "Guilty."

# 6.

# WHAT THE INTERNET MEANS TO *YOU*

Let's face it; the Internet is a fact of life for nearly everyone at this point. When I was employed by a corporation, I logged on in the morning and stayed on all day long—primarily to remain "accessible" for the deluge of mostly unwanted e-mail messages.

It still amazes me how people in a business network gravitate to every new form of communication. I can still remember how fascinated we all were with voice mail when we first got it, leaving an incredible number of unnecessary messages and making sure that the maximum number of people were included by adding their phone numbers to each. It wasn't until we noticed that there were far fewer receptionists and secretaries employed that we realized that we had eliminated *people* as well as those pesky, pink "While You Were Out" telephone slips.

With the advent of e-mail, we had the opportunity to "copy" even more people who didn't really want "info copies" of our self-aggrandizement. And it was made even easier to inundate all of those hapless souls by creating address lists that could be accessed by just the click of a mouse.

As someone suddenly unemployed, it is critical that you DO NOT look at the Internet as your friend. You know in your heart (and from experience—possibly one that *got* you in the situation you are currently experiencing) that it is too easy to spend too much time "surfing the net" when you should be doing more productive things like looking for a job or cleaning the windows. However, if you persist in using it (under the guise of "research" or "checking my e-mail messages"), limit yourself by placing an old-fashioned, wind-up alarm clock next to the monitor of your computer, and set the alarm to go off at a specified time.

The advent of "smart" phones has increased the possibility of abusing the Internet/e-mail and, especially, text messaging capabilities in recent years. It does make you more accessible, but it also provides just one more distraction from the job that you were originally hired to do. Keep it in your pocket or purse and check for messages and information as appropriate, rather than responding to the ring tone. People *are* watching.

Trust me on this.

# 7.

# THE HAPPY WANDERER

I once heard a physician describe children with attention deficit disorder as "happy wanderers" because they can't stay focused on individual tasks for an extended period of time. They tend to move from one thing to the next as their interest, or patience, wanes and spend the day wonderfully discovering new things and leaving a trail of uncompleted tasks.

In the "working world" I was a slave to "task completion." This was confounded by incessant telephone calls and hastily called meetings, which interfered with bringing closure to a specific project before I could move on to the next. Industry has a lexicon that includes terms such as "action items," which are assigned to individuals in meetings to be concluded before the *next* meeting. Gee, I almost forgot how much my life revolved around meetings … I'll have to call one for myself and see if I can still maintain an agenda.

Being suddenly unemployed means that you may find yourself becoming a happy wanderer—and that's not bad— but you need to put it in perspective. I can start the day with a specific task and find myself wandering up to the laundry to throw a load into the washer and then pausing to snap on the television (this is another area to be considered seriously) to, ostensibly, find out what is going on in the world (mostly talk shows where an incredible number of dysfunctional people discuss some of the strangest behaviors known to man) and then moving on to arrange the magazines on the coffee table. This movement from one thing to another can lead to entire mornings being spent doing nothing really—or even remotely—worthwhile.

I sometimes wonder if I have an undiagnosed case of attention deficit disorder.

# 8.

## PETS

This is a critical area for someone who is unemployed and spending the day at home. Fortunately, we are blessed with two geriatric dogs, four cats (one of whom is seventeen), five goldfish, and three horses. This means that I have a constant motion requirement at the front door of the house. There is always *someone* who wants to either come in or go out (well, not the horses and goldfish—but they have other needs) all day long. The geriatric portion of my pet kingdom means that I am also given the opportunity—on a daily basis—to clean up after them. Here's a hint: BUY ONE OF THOSE MINI CARPET CLEANERS IF YOU HAVE OLD PETS. I am the king of spot cleaning the carpet. I defer to no man, or woman, on this!

# 9.

# THE CLASSIFIEDS

Before I became suddenly unemployed, the classified section of the newspaper—especially the Sunday paper—was scanned only when things were going badly at work or if the corporation was exhibiting signs of fiscal distress. After I was liberated to find a new avenue in life, the classifieds became a major part of my week. I paced myself, avoiding the daily listings, and concentrated on the Sunday offerings, usually waiting until Monday morning to read them from beginning to end.

Usually, I would arm myself with a yellow highlighter and a pen to make comments on the margins of high-lighted items. And, after outlining promising possibilities, I would carefully cut them out of the paper with scissors and attach them with tape to blank sheets of typing paper. I even created an "employment file" with tabbed sections to indicate job offerings to which I responded, with copies of correspondence sent to prospective employers. I was being very businesslike in my approach.

As time wore on, my file grew larger, and my analysis of the classifieds became more detailed. This was personal research and marketing at its finest. Never mind that I had always been told that "the best jobs never appear in the paper," which was probably something invented by personnel agencies to make a naive public believe that they held the answer to unemployment woes. After several months, and a relatively huge file, I began to suspect that something was amiss in my strategy.

I was getting a lot of "hits" (usually postcards that acknowledged receipt of my precious resume), but not many warm responses from firms seriously interested in my presence at an interview. Something was wrong—either in my approach or in the very nature of the process. Going back to the proverbial drawing board, I carefully reviewed and analyzed my "database" (the big fat file) and determined that getting to an interview by responding to the classifieds is a lot like sending out a survey—a response rate of 5 percent would be phenomenal, and mine was *less* than that!

I still have the big file, which is dwindling as I use its contents to start fires in the woodstove. I have ceased making the U.S. Postal Service richer one first-class stamp at a time. And I have relegated myself to a weekly scan of the classifieds only in areas that interest me. I have, however, made some observations regarding the *language* of the classifieds that may come in handy for those intrepid souls who have become suddenly unemployed and want to take a whack at frustrating their efforts.

# 10.

## DECODING THOSE CLASSIFIEDS

Here's one that always gets my attention and a laugh:

*"Looking for a motivated problem solver to work in our challenging, fast-paced distribution environment. Must have excellent organizational skills and computer skills and be comfortable working with numbers. Qualified candidate must have good phone skills and be able to work effectively with others."*

What I love about this one is that they don't use the word "secretary" anywhere in the ad. Any time the terms "excellent organizational skills" are coupled with "phone skills," please plan on being offered a desk in the lobby and just a tad more than minimum wage.

Truth, it seems, is stranger than fiction when it comes to the classifieds. A review of actual ads netted some real beauties:

### MARKETING REPRESENTATIVE
*Local, fast-growing firm seeks self-motivated, goal-oriented individual for our daytime marketing department.*

*Duties will include servicing present clients and to aggressively seek new business relationships. Salary plus commission. For more info call xxx-xxxx.*

I didn't call, but I was curious. Do they have a nighttime marketing department? And what kind of *servicing* did they have in mind?

## TECHNICIAN
*We are looking for A+ certified technicians. Must be able to work 1st and 2nd shift. Must have at least 6 mos. - 1 yr. on the job exp. If you've had a Security Clearance, that is a huge plus.*

The above was from an employment agency. The brevity and use of abbreviation always makes me think that the agency must have a budgetary formula tied to the commission that the agency will collect from the employer.

## CUSTOMER SERVICE
*Growing business has created a need for full- and part-time Customer Service positions at both our East and West Shore stores. Work in pleasant surroundings for the areas fastest growing furniture store. Fax resume to xxx-xxxx.*

Why, oh why, can't these people just place their ad in the **SALES** category of the classifieds? Maybe the "pleasant surroundings" mean that you can sit on the furniture when you aren't performing customer service?

## OFFICE ADMINISTRATOR
*#1 Real Estate office in the area is looking for an individual with management experience to assist in the operation of the company. This individual must be self-motivated and dependable. Must be able to work well with over eighty agents and supervise staff members. Experience with office equipment, computer hardware/software, and website design/maintenance is required. Must be able to multi-task and prioritize. This is a great opportunity for a qualified person looking for long-term employment with a*

*growing company. Please fax your resume and salary requirements to xxx-xxxx.*

Deal with eighty real estate agents, and maintain the website? I wonder if the company provides free-choice medication to the multi-tasking prioritizer that they hire!

## DEVELOPMENT ASSOCIATE

*Three positions available! Twelve week temporary position with high-profile, non-profit organization. If you are looking for an opportunity to develop your professional skills, this is the opportunity for you! This project will require self-motivation, flexibility, and excellent communication skills. You will interact with diverse companies and individuals. Training provided. College degree preferred. Valid driver's license and availability of personal auto required. Salary $11-13/hr DOE. Please forward your resume to: xxxxx@xxxxxxx.xxx*

Can you say *telemarketer*? Can you say *fundraising*? Can you say *recent college graduates* who can't find a job?

## WANTED EXPERIENCED BUSINESS PROFESSIONALS

*Our business is booming, we're Xxxxx International, the world's #1 business coaching team. Call to see if you qualify to be a business coach and franchisee. xxx-xxxx*

Actually, this one brought back a memory. I did respond to a similar ad and met some guy from Chicago in a motel room for an interview. After glancing at my resume, he said that I was qualified to attend his company's training seminar and that I would be responsible for my own transportation and lodging in the Windy City during the week-long session. Somehow, the prospect of a week of indoctrination and pitch for a franchise fee didn't appeal.

## HUMAN SERVICES

*Full time, flexible schedules. Great benefits. Own vehicle. Call xxx-xxxx, ext. xxx.*

I really liked this ad. It's concise, punchy, and conveys a certain mystery. The prospect of working in "human services" while I drive my own car makes me wonder what it really entails. Cab driver? Home healthcare? Prostitution? I didn't call.

Actually, I have found that the automobile classifieds are sometimes more interesting than the employment ads. Perhaps the creative types at the newspaper would be better served to write employment ads that followed the format of the vehicle variety. I *know* that I would respond to one that went:

*WANTED: Solid performer, power everything, high performance engine, must have overdrive. Mileage and body not a factor if in good shape. $50,000 per year OBO. Send or e-mail resume ASAP - no phone calls please.*

I'd LOVE to see the resumes that appeared on the doorstep of a prospective employer who used this ad.

# 11.

# THE POWER OF OBSERVATION

When you are unemployed, it is possible to enhance your powers of observation, due largely to the fact that you are no longer narrowly focused on your career. Testing these newly amplified powers requires perseverance and an ability to divorce yourself from thinking about your past job and allowing anger to shorten your perspective. Allow yourself to expand and let your senses absorb your surroundings (God, this sounds like one of those self-help books, doesn't it?). You will see more things to which you can apply your sense of wonder, some worthwhile, many absurd.

Recently, I was walking past a dumpster and noticed a box sticking out of the top of the partially open lid. It wasn't that the box had colorful graphics or an attractive color, but rather, it had a message that drew my attention. On the box it said, "Do It Yourself Success Kit." Wow! What an opportunity for a suddenly unemployed person with a newly enhanced sense of awareness. The possibilities leapt through my brain. Could this be a sign? Could it be the proverbial message in the bottle that we all seek?

Carefully, I approached the dumpster. Glancing about, I made sure that no one who knew me would see me rooting through the trash in a public receptacle (there's a classic episode of *Seinfeld* in which George Costanza is surprised by his future mother-in-law while retrieving and eating a chocolate éclair from the kitchen trash. I didn't want to make something like that a real-life experience for myself). I carefully rescued the cardboard from its companions and looked inside. Nothing. There wasn't even a company name that would give me a reason to search the Internet or the telephone directories for the true meaning of this enclosure for the salvation of the unemployed. I regretfully returned the box to its erstwhile home and continued on my way, pondering the possibilities. Perhaps there was a meaning to this exercise if I simply applied my sense of wonder to it.

I have always prided myself on being a consummate do-it-yourselfer. I change the oil in the car. I repair furniture that has loose glue joints. I build shelves in closets. I repainted the house. Why couldn't *I* create my own do it yourself success kit?

Returning home, I applied myself to the task (well, I *am* unemployed, and we are allowed to do things like this) with a yellow legal pad and a number 2 wooden pencil. At the top of the page I wrote "Do It Yourself Success Kit" and then sat and pondered for about a half hour.

What is success? Is it making more money than you can spend in a lifetime? Is it receiving adulation from the multitudes? Is it running faster or throwing a ball better than anyone else in the game? Is it creating something that will make the memory of you, as an individual, live on beyond your allotted span? Or is it finding your own happiness? I realized that personal success is based upon having a goal and that a do it yourself success kit would need a goal as the key element.

This process brought back memories of junior high guidance counselors, college career workshops, countless career seminars, written statements of interest and aspiration (a new one each time I was transferred to a different corporate division) and, finally, recent outplacement workshops we unemployed types were required to attend. What the hell *was* my goal?

Pondering for another half hour (try doing *that* while working for a hard-nosed divisional vice president!), I came to the conclusion that my long-range goal was to be happy (I wrote it down), and my immediate goal was to find some kind of employment that would put food on the table. These two goals, at times, seem mutually exclusive. Would I be willing to sacrifice my happiness for money?

I began to write down things that made me happy and was amazed at the length of the list. Then I began to write down things I know that I can do that might possibly make some money, or possible employers who might hire me based upon my skills. The list of money makers was lamentably shorter than the list of things that made me happy. For instance, I don't really think that a ski resort would hire me because I really enjoy skiing—besides, it's pretty seasonal when you live in Pennsylvania.

For some reason, I held the lists up and placed them side by side. A little light went on, and I committed them to text on the computer—column A and column B—and printed it out. Then I took my trusty pencil (ever notice how anyone who ever worked for a newspaper or a magazine prefers a pencil to a pen?) and began to draw lines from the happy items to the moneymakers/employment items—just like those matching tests in grade school. I was surprised at the number of connections, multiple connections in some cases, which I could make between being happy and making money. Admittedly, some of them were *real* stretches, but it was a good exercise in beginning to make my own do it yourself success kit.

Try it. It may not get you a job, but it will help you believe in yourself.

# 12.

## GROWING A BEARD

Sudden unemployment and the removal from the mainstream often lends itself to experimentation in facial hair if you are a man—a perfect time to grow a beard if you haven't done so in a while. If you can get past the itchy stage, and if you have the ability to grow a good one, you should indulge yourself. Unlike the beard or moustache you attempt during vacation, the one that good sense tells you to shave off on Monday morning before you return to work, facial hair allows you to exude a ruddy sense of individualism. It's a great time to experiment with your new-found freedom. Besides, if you decide it's just not "you," it can be shaved off at a later date. Other experiments in personal freedom, like tattoos, can be more problematic as you transition back into the working world since they aren't as easily removed. If going with a tattoo, get one that can be obscured by clothing during the interview. Since you can't foretell who will be interviewing you for the next position, the ability to return to "normal" mode is critical.

# 13.

## THE NEIGHBORS

I was fortunate, at first, in having a next-door neighbor who became suddenly unemployed at the same time as I did (he has since become employed by another corporation and is very happy being back in the groove). I made it a point to walk my son out to the school bus stop and wait with the other mothers (yes, mothers—I was the only man there) for the big, yellow bus to pick up the kids. This has given me a greater appreciation for my mother, who was a stay-at-home mom in the 1950s and 60s. As kids, we would wave good-bye to my father as he left for work in the morning and greet him when he came home in the evening. This allowed us to create a living hell for my mother (especially in the summer) by making her the totem for all childhood demands.

The mothers in my neighborhood are primarily stay-at-home moms with small children—an anachronism in today's world—who make me appreciate the thankless task that it is at times. We had conversations about gardening, the weather, what time the Cub Scout meeting will be, and other assorted domesticities. Unlike the previous world in which I existed, we never discussed who is doing whom, what a complete turd the new divisional vice president is, or speculation on what the percentage is for the next merit raise.

It's a very congenial existence, and I sometimes wonder if the neighbors think of me as "the happy idiot" rather than "the happy wanderer."

# 14.

## WRITE IT DOWN

Anyone who has become unemployed fantasizes. We fantasize about what we *really* should have said when the ax fell. We fantasize about how much we're missed by our coworkers and how the organization is probably faltering because of our absence. We fantasize about fantastic new things that we are going to accomplish with our new-found freedom.

The truth of the matter is, we really end up floundering in a mixture of suppressed rage and occasional self-pity while we attempt to set our course in a new direction. One of my favorite authors, Jimmy Buffett, said in his autobiography that he was absolutely in awe of another author, Herman Wouk, because he has maintained a daily diary since 1948. That's a pretty telling statement from the man from Margaritaville. Incidentally, Jimmy Buffett is not recommended reading for those unemployed people who are *really* living in a fantasy world. Unless you are willing to work very, very hard at seeming carefree, ol' Jim is not the person to use as your role model.

However, the diary part has much merit. It's an excellent discipline to write down everything you do for an entire day, noting times and comparing it to an agenda that you have set for yourself the day before (or, at least, that morning). It is truly amazing how much time we manage to fart away and the amount of time we can't account for in a day's measured length. When you are "working" and know that, no matter what, you'll get paid for it, the amount of time spent seems somewhat academic. No matter what rate you observe, hourly, weekly, biweekly, bimonthly, monthly ... there is always a goof-off factor involved. Time spent in the hall talking about Monday night football, time spent e-mailing bad jokes, time spent handling family matters on the phone—are all factored into your inevitable paycheck.

When you are suddenly unemployed, you have a lot of time on your hands and no one to account for it but yourself. My wife noticed that not long after I became unemployed, I had discarded the habit of looking over my shoulder (really!) before responding to a question or making a statement (the company I worked for made you really paranoid about being "spied upon" the last year and a half that I worked there, since business was really going into the dumpster). With all that time on your hands, you'll find yourself squandering it like found money until you realize that you're not making as much as you had been.

Write it down. You'll be amazed.

# 15.

# THE CONCRETE JUNGLE

I have tried, religiously, to avoid living "in town." Not because I have a phobia about cities, but because I was raised in the country and simply prefer the somewhat wider, more open, spaces provided there. God knows, I've worn out any number of cars and done my share of depleting the fossil fuel reserves commuting to the city to make a living. I just haven't spent much time living in one.

The time I have spent in cities across the United States has given me an appreciation of the benefits of city living. San Francisco's BART public transportation is probably the finest, and most reasonable, method of conveying yourself from one place to another that I have ever encountered. I spent the better part of a week in Nashville once and never rented a car. As a matter of fact, I walked to nearly everything I wanted to see. If you can afford it, staying in downtown Washington, D.C. is a "city experience" that requires little public transportation. I really envy my urban brethren, their proximity to attractions, and their workplaces. That is, unless they have become unemployed and need to find a new path to gainful occupation. In that case, we are all brothers and sisters placing one foot before the other on the pavement of joblessness.

A friend of mine made a go of freelance writing and finally concluded that steady employment was preferable to the vagaries of publishers who sat on manuscripts for months at a time and then, at best, issued kill fees on prose he deemed deathless. He took a job with the federal government in Baltimore, thinking that it would simplify his life. In an office overlooking the Inner Harbor of that fair city, he extolled the virtues of strolling the promenade on his lunch hour and absorbing the view of the water. He also had to live in a suburb of Baltimore, because it was within his financial means and traveled downtown to earn his keep. As a result, his means of financial security was protected, but the commute sucked.

Another friend recounted his commute to Manhattan during the fifteen years he worked there. "I lived in Wayne, New Jersey, because I couldn't afford to live in Manhattan; drove each morning to the train station, took the train, took the subway, and then walked six blocks to the office. I spent nearly two and a half hours a day commuting across the river!" He later began looking for a job in Pennsylvania and had trouble getting hired, because employers didn't want to offer him a cut in salary. "I had a hell of a time convincing someone that I was *willing* to take less money, because I'd be further ahead financially by *not* working in Manhattan and spending over twelve hours a week commuting!"

I don't know if there's a moral here. Perhaps it would be: working for a living is damned inconvenient, no matter where you live.

A good possible exercise at this point—if you are living (and formerly working) in a city environment—would be to enumerate the positives and the negatives of your dilemma. For example:

**Positives**

Public transportation: It's cheaper than owning or using a car, by far.

Proximity to people in the same predicament: If you live in the country, you have to travel about to find other people who are unemployed. In the city, you can just walk down the street.

## Negatives

Proximity to people in the same predicament: You're so darn accessible to all of those other people who want to tell you their tale of woe!

Employers know where you live: They know you'll look at whatever they have to offer, because you don't want to, or can't, move. Actually, this holds true for people living in the country, too.

When you've made the list, compare it to what's available out there, and adjust your strategy accordingly.

# 16.

## PLACES TO AVOID

When you are steadily employed, you generally have a place, or a number of places, that you like to be when you aren't "working." One of my favorite places used to be on the riding lawnmower. I really enjoyed the soothing hum of the motor, no interruptions (yeah, like who *wants* to mow your lawn for you?), no telephone and, best of all, no thinking. Well, there was some thinking going on, but it was mostly planning for the future. I remember that I used to look out of the office window at the landscape contractor's employees mowing those vast expanses with envy. They (1) got to work in the outdoors, (2) didn't have to answer a telephone, and (3) at the end of the day they could see *exactly* what they did. Heaven, huh?

Then I became suddenly unemployed and found that riding the lawnmower was suddenly one of the places I really didn't want to be. Sitting on that weapon of agrarian destruction with nothing to do but mow grass allowed me to stew on my predicament and build scenarios, which only increased my rage. Fortunately, I was "downsized" in October. So was the grass.

Another place to avoid is whatever restaurant you used to go to at lunchtime with the other people from "work." There's either an active avoidance by the regulars or a falsely cheerful interest in "how you're doing" and "how much they are thinking about you." Hell, they aren't thinking about *you*, they're silently thinking about how glad they are that it wasn't *them*. They are whistling as they pass your graveyard.

Another thing to expect, when you least expect it, is bumping into someone with whom you have worked in a public place with. The first time it happened to me I was in a local building supply store and bumped into a woman with whom I worked and spoke to on an almost daily basis. On seeing her, I smiled and walked in her direction only to be given the blank look you give a complete stranger in the middle of a shopping mall. She walked right past, within two feet of me, giving no indication that she had ever seen me before in her life! In her defense, I *was* wearing a baseball cap. (Sure, that must have been what it was, I mean, who could ever forget *me*?)

Thankfully, there hasn't been any real effort made to begin something like a class-action suit, or create a "network" of similarly unemployed people. Really! Who wants to network with a bunch of people who were let go from that same place? I think you'd get better results if you joined a model railroad club.

# 17.

## OUTPLACEMENT SERVICES

Here is possibly the greatest scam currently available in the corporate world. Big companies, in a sincere effort to avoid lawsuits initiated by employees they have terminated, hire "outplacement specialists" to guide the employees through this difficult transition. I'm sure that firms offering these services have a variety of arguments to justify their existence and an equal number of indignant responses to anyone questioning their necessity in the litigious world in which we live, but I just can't see it.

The company from which I abruptly departed offered a two-day seminar by an outplacement firm, which was—unbelievably—*mandatory* if you wanted to file an unemployment claim! The sessions were led by a woman with a strident manner of addressing the problem at hand. She dominated the meetings by recalling her experience with downsizing and encouraging us to perform written exercises in a large binder that was supplied by her company. Imagine, if you will, a room full of extremely disgruntled people (the guy who had relocated from California to Pennsylvania only two months previously got the nod from the group as "most likely to commit a felonious act") being led by a cheerleader paid by the company that not only fired them, but was making them sit in a room under duress. It was not pretty.

Here's a suggestion to employers "doing the downsize tango": Take the large amount of money you are planning on giving the outplacement service, divide it equally among the employees to be terminated (along with a liability release form), and give each employee a list of local personnel agencies (free) and a subscription to the Sunday newspaper (cheap).

The employees get approximately the same results as they would have with the outplacement firm and have more money to tide them over until they find something else.

# 18.

# WHAT OTHER PEOPLE DO FOR A LIVING

Here's a subject that both the employed and the unemployed ponder on a regular basis when first being introduced to someone new or even seeing someone interesting on the street. This becomes more intensely scrutinized when you are suddenly unemployed. One of my favorites—years ago while making the half-hour commute each day to work—was to see some guy who appeared to be about twenty-three years old, driving a BMW and talking on a cell phone. My mental question was, invariably, "what does *that* guy do for a living?" Since that time, everyone seems to have a cell phone, and I have concluded that he was probably spending everything he had on a car lease. Since I am older, and suddenly unemployed, my musings on the subject of other people's jobs have become more far-reaching and border on the abstract.

I now watch people on the television and wonder what some of them do to make ends meet. One of my favorites in this regard is Jesse Jackson. Anytime there seems to be a crisis in the world that becomes a media event, ol' Jesse seems to appear. This, in itself, is commendable. If there was a possibility for *me* to mediate an international dispute, I wouldn't hesitate to get on the first flight I could book. There is one question in my mind: "who *pays* for the airplane, the hotel, the meals, and the car rental?" I can't believe that the Reverend Jackson is doing this out of his own pocket. Compounding this personal analysis is a personal sense of wonder regarding *how* he makes a living. Does he preach somewhere on a regular basis? Has he made some incredibly successful investments? Did he marry someone with a lot of family money? HOW does he do it? I want to know!

Other people who occasionally occupy my thoughts in this regard are David Cassidy and Connie Stevens. And where the heck is Bobby Sherman, and what is *he* doing for a living now?

A number of years ago I went to hear a lecture by Louis Rukeyser, the host of *Wall $treet Week*, sponsored by the Junior League (who else???). There is no question in my mind that this guy was well employed. But, after nearly two hours of his discourse, a gentleman seated next to me leaned over and said, "I hear that they gave this guy thirty grand to speak tonight." *Thirty thousand dollars* to give a speech, which most of the audience didn't understand and provided absolutely no stock tips? This is *real* employment, my friends. Where do I sign up?

This kind of speculation and fantasizing is not a useful practice for the suddenly unemployed and should *never* be used as a conversational gambit in a job interview.

# 19.

## A SENSE OF WONDER

We all wonder about various arcane things, unemployed or not. However, when you are suddenly unemployed you have the God-given right to wonder about anything, at any time—largely because you have the time on your hands to wonder about things! Some of the things that come to mind are probably too embarrassing to share with even your close friends, since they would think that you have lost whatever mind you had when you "fit into" the "working" world. For example, I wonder what William Shatner looks like when he gets up in the morning. Does he have his hair on one of those Styrofoam things on a dressing table? And can you imagine what sort of conversation occurs when Bill and Hillary Clinton are alone—if they ever are? What did the friends of The Artist Formerly Known as Prince call him when they saw him during that phase of his career? (Oddly enough, his real first name *is* Prince; I learned that when I used the Internet to find out what his real name was.) Maybe they just held up that symbol he used during that period to get his attention. Does Frank Sinatra Jr. really think that he would have had a singing career if his paternity had been otherwise? Why did they make U.S. paper currency green? If this computer that I'm using cost $2,000 four years ago, why does it cost $599 now? And, following that same logic, why does the same make and model of the car I purchased in 1991 for $17,000 cost $35,000 now?

See? This is why you should keep your sense of wonder to yourself, especially when you are unemployed. Just think of it as your little secret.

# 20.

## DEALING WITH YOUR PARENTS

When you are suddenly unemployed, your parents are generally the ones who are most concerned outside of your immediate household. I think that they (although they would never admit it) feel as though they have failed somehow. This is particularly true of baby boomers that have been suddenly downsized from a large corporation. When our parents began their working careers, it was assumed that whomever or whatever they worked for would provide the stability and environment for a long and successful working career. The phone company was always touted as "the place to get a job" when I was a kid. It was big, everybody had a phone, and if you started working there, you *couldn't* lose your job unless you were convicted of a felony; it was ideal job security.

I distinctly remember when I took the job that I was suddenly unemployed from, my father said, "That's a good place to work. You should plan on staying there for a while —like thirty years." This was the same man who said to me when I was about twelve years old, "If a man hasn't made it in this world by the time he's forty, he should just fold up his pocketknife and put it back in his pocket."

I really didn't plan on staying where I was for thirty years. Hell, I didn't see myself staying there for thirty *months* after the first couple of weeks there, but I managed to stretch it out to sixteen years. And the pocketknife thing just didn't help my ego much when I had my fortieth birthday.

If there's a moral here, it would be to carefully consider what you tell your children about life, because they probably *are* listening.

# 21.
## PART-TIME JOBS

When the unemployment checks cease coming, along with the possible offers of meaningful employment, it's time to keep the wolves at bay with part-time employment.

I scanned the classified ads in the newspaper after reading the business page (which carried an article about record-*low* levels of unemployment—apparently they weren't aware of the spike in the statistics regarding males in their late 40s). I got in the car to look for part-time employment. Picking up applications at several large, home-building supply companies and learning that the wages offered were barely above federally mandated minimums, I headed for home to fill in the necessary information to return to the world of the wage-earner. On my way I noticed a billboard that fairly shouted "We want *you* to become a member of *our* team!" They were also offering twelve bucks an hour for what seemed to be mental-midget work.

Wheeling into the parking lot of this major truck carrier of packages, I had visions of doing a degree of physical work, for better than average compensation, with no commitment to a career. I parked the car and walked through the security gate, which had large signs stating that all employees were subject to "pat down" upon leaving the premises. I went to the personnel office (yes, they *do* call it "personnel" and not "human resources") and filled out an application. I was asked to prove that I could pick up a sixty pound box (which I did) and was told that I would be notified when I could come to work. Wow, somebody actually *wanted* to hire me, and they were offering a hundred dollar bonus if you stayed with the company for the first forty hours of work!

The people in the security office made me empty my pockets and "patted me down" (yet another "first" in life experiences) before I could go into the parking lot to get my car.

I agreed to take the "sunrise" shift, which started at 4:30 a.m. and ran until they were out of packages to unload or 10:00 a.m.—whichever came first. And after a brief training session, which consisted primarily of videos showing how to correctly pick up cardboard cartons in a tractor-trailer and place them on a conveyor belt, I was sent out to try my hand at unloading trucks.

My first clue regarding the nature of the work was written faintly in white crayon at the edge of the loading dock door. "*Welcome to Hell*" had been inscribed for posterity by another hapless soul who apparently thought they were going to get the big bucks for a little physical effort. I had no idea how prophetic that simple phrase was to prove over the next few hours. My experience with package delivery prior to this point had consisted of taking a cardboard carton from some nice person in a clean delivery truck and signing my name on a proffered clipboard.

These damn trucks had cardboard cartons of all sizes jammed in them floor-to-ceiling, as well as tires, wooden pallets, truck hitches, rolled carpets, bags of envelopes, plastic pails, containers labeled as hazardous materials, eight-foot-long mini-blinds, bicycles, chain saws, and large boxes with yellow warning tape on them, which indicated that the contents weighed one hundred plus pounds. Whatever happened to that nice box in the personnel office that was about a one foot square and weighed sixty pounds? It sure wasn't on *this* trailer.

After performing my duties for several hours on the docks (where the temperature was approximately 90 degrees) and losing about five pounds through sweating, I was told by the supervisor that I was "done for the day" and could "clock out" (again, another "first" in my life-experience portfolio). I have always prided myself on being in pretty good physical condition, but after this episode, I began to have doubts about it. I dragged myself, soaking wet with sweat, to the security building where I emptied my pockets and was "patted down" by the security guy (I found out later that if a woman was on duty, she simply waved one of those electronic wands, like they have at airport gates, over my physique) and was sent on my less-than-merry way.

Subsequent days were carbon copies of the first, and some were even worse, but I was *employed* and making twelve bucks an hour!

An amusing phase of the job, which lasted nearly six months before my wife insisted that I cease working there (due to the resemblance I had to a zombie after the first three months) occurred in the first few days. As I unloaded trucks in the sweltering atmosphere, a supervisor would stop by occasionally and ask, "How are you doing?" I, in my naïveté, assumed that he was really concerned about my progress, until I looked around at the other employees and realized that I was the oldest guy working there. It wasn't that he was being solicitous, but rather, was concerned that the gray-haired guy was going to drop dead on *his* shift.

# 22.

## THANK GOD I'M A COUNTRY BOY

I have had the good fortune to have been raised in the country on a farm that never supported our family without my father working in the city operating an insurance brokerage, but a farm nevertheless. Since then I have always tried to live outside of cities, although I have had to work in them to earn my keep. My wife was raised in the suburbs where all of your companions could walk to your house and school. This is probably the major functional difference in our upbringing and has sometimes led to a lack of understanding regarding human interaction.

When you are unemployed, you find that you have the *time* to talk to your neighbors, and if you are country-raised, having a conversation has certain rules of etiquette that must be observed if you are to maintain your relationship with the other country folk.

"Why can't you just *ask* someone a simple question?" she says.

I reply, "You have to go through the formalities before you can get to the point of why you stopped by."

"I don't understand why it takes you a half hour to ask some guy if he is willing to come and mow the hay field," she says.

"It's because he doesn't see me more than a half-dozen times a year, and we have to 'catch up' before we can get down to business," I reply.

Our neighbor, Jason, is a full-time farmer and a member of a fairly conservative Mennonite Church (which is kind of like being Amish, except that you get to use tractors and drive cars instead of a horse and buggy). He is a deeply religious man with a farm and about eleven kids and annually makes hay for us on the field across the road from our house. This past year I went to see him about this project (boy, is *this* worlds apart from getting in the car and going to work for a corporation), and I began the conversation by asking him how his father was doing.

"Well," he responded, "he's doing better than he was since he got out of the hospital."

This, of course, required further inquiry on my part regarding the nature of his dad's illness and gaining the knowledge that his father suffered from Parkinson's disease. He continued his description of the incident that sent his father to the local hospital, which included informing me that "he was doing poorly, and we took him to the doctor's office where they took his blood pressure, and he didn't have any." He continued, "That really got the doctor's attention, and he called for an ambulance to come fetch Dad to the hospital where they put him on a machine, which got his blood going again. It's a miracle that he's alive and didn't suffer any brain damage from it." I, of course, expressed amazement that the old man was still alive and functioning, to which Jason replied, "There must have been enough blood left in his brain that it just kinda 'drizzled down' through there and kept enough oxygen going through it that he didn't suffer any lasting damage."

I love the fact that someone can look at something as fragile as a human life and equate it to something like the loss of oil pressure in a tractor without ruining the bearings in the engine. It's just the kind of conversation that makes me wonder how, before I was suddenly unemployed, I managed to sit through all of those incredibly dull meetings in conference rooms where the most important topics of discussion were things like how to increase capacity on stamping machines in Mexico to reduce the backlog in our orders.

# 23.

## CAPTAIN OBVIOUS AND DEPRESSION IN THE CITY

I am often accused by close friends and, more so, by members of my family of overstating the facts in conversations. This is possibly due to the degree of time I have spent alone while researching new avenues of possible employment. My son summed up one of my monologues, after listening patiently while I reviewed whatever brilliant piece of enlightening information I had gleaned by declaring, "Thank you, Captain Obvious!"

It was a humbling moment. And one that made me aware of the fact that others in my circle probably find me incredibly boring at times—particularly when I have had too much time to dwell upon my predicament. Needless to say, it's enlightening yet depressing to learn.

In my intellectual wanderings, I ran across a study regarding depression and downward mobility, published in the *Journal of Epidemiology and Community Health*, which shows that findings suggest that women's risk of depression is tied to social class at birth, while men's risk of depression is more closely linked to social status at midlife. This was one fact-finding mission that I wasn't going to share with others until I could condense it into some sort of a terse statement that wouldn't make me seem like, well, Captain Obvious.

Further reading in the article revealed that the study was conducted in England where researchers followed the lives of 503 men and women who were born in 1947 to mothers living in Newcastle upon Tyne in the northeast portion of that country. The results showed that, overall, more women than men were depressed at age fifty, and twice as many women as men reported moving down in social class since birth. However, men who became downwardly mobile were 3.5 times more likely to be depressed than women who became downwardly mobile.

Now, the first question that came to mind was: who on earth funded a study that lasted over *fifty years*? Particularly a study about depression in an industrial city in England? And how much did a study of that magnitude cost? Duh! *I* could have told them (at great length and with grandiose degrees of repetition) that people who are downwardly mobile (can you say unemployed?) become depressed—for a helluva lot less money than was spent on the study!

Captain Obvious, indeed.

# 24.

# THE RESUME

I have often wondered why "resume" became the popular title of this dreaded document. It can be called "curriculum vitae" (which instantly identifies you, I think, as a college student looking for a first job or a desperately aging philosophy professor who never achieved tenure), but "resume" is the term most often employed. In the case of the suddenly unemployed person, the significance of the word without the acceptably absent accent mark indicates to a prospective employer that you are willing to continue your working life.

As an employed person, I have written countless resumes over the years, many of which were sent out to persons or companies looking for someone apparently just like me. Strangely, most were unwilling to settle for the real thing, given the number of letters regretfully declining my offer to join their organization. The letters responding to my inquiries usually began with "although your credentials are impressive" and ended with "we will keep your resume on file for six months." Is that six-month thing a federal law? Why don't they keep them for a year or tell you that they tossed the encapsulation of your life's work in the trash after reading it? I suppose that someone in "human resources" could tell me where that six-month rule came from, but I really don't care after seeing it at the end of a rejection.

When you are suddenly unemployed, you begin to look at your resume in a new light. No longer is it a simple shot in the dark at a possible improvement in your working life. It becomes a medium for you to communicate your value to a possible employer. You can buy or borrow from the library literally thousands of books on how to write resumes. I find it hard to believe that there are *that* many book publishers out there who are willing to pay people to write essentially the same thing over and over. For God's sake, it's a resume—not an art form.

As an unemployed person, you should be aware of a few things when writing a resume:

1. Make sure that you have your name, address (home and e-mail), and telephone number on the damn thing.
2. Exaggerate wildly.
3. Remember that all your former employer can basically do is verify that you were employed there for the time period specified on your resume (although I suspect that many former employers provide hints during inquiries that you are just slightly more acceptable than Adolf Hitler as an employment prospect).
4. Make certain that you don't provide any dates that would easily allow your age to be determined if you are over forty.
5. If you provide references, call them and coach them on what to say if they are contacted regarding your qualities as a human being. Better yet, give them a freaking script to read.

I don't know if any of the above can be guaranteed to get you an interview, but hey, you're unemployed, and the worst that can happen is that you'll get a letter telling you that "although your credentials are impressive ..."

# 25.

# INTERVIEWS

Based upon the believability of your resume, you should get some interviews. If you are suddenly unemployed and on the far side of forty without a specific career skill, like engineering or orthopedic surgery, you won't get too many. However, the interviews you *do* get should be treated with gravity if you think you have a shot at getting the position offered. On the bright side, it's an opportunity to hone your skills and match wits with a person who thinks you just might fit into an organization. On the down side, you are probably competing with a number of younger people who are willing to work for less than you are.

The first few interviews, if it's been a long time since you have gone through the process, can be exhausting and leave you with a feeling that you may have either said too much, waffled a bit on the job experience, or said too little about what the interviewer really wanted to hear. My wife, who has interviewed a lot of prospective employees, has a rule of thumb when responding to a job in the classifieds. "If they say that they are looking for someone with specific experience in a given area, don't apply if you don't have it."

She also told me, "If you don't know what an acronym in the ad means, *don't bother applying!*"

I once responded to a classified ad that required familiarity with a spreadsheet program, and, since I had taken a company-sponsored, eight-hour training class in the subject two years previously, I said I was familiar with it. I was granted an interview and appeared for it wearing a nice suit and carrying my leather portfolio. The interview went swimmingly (well, *I* thought it did) until the interviewer requested that I take a proficiency test on the required program. Rather than retire from the field, I bravely said, "Sure!" and spent the following half hour sweating in front of a computer whose program grilled me on my knowledge of the subject. Searching my memory, I did battle with the computer and actually managed to get a score that proclaimed me "proficient" in the subject.

I never heard from them again.

Several phrases that have brought me closer to the interviewer and occasionally have resulted in agitated note-taking on the interview sheet are:

"I consider myself a team player and really miss being a part of a team."

"No, I don't mind traveling."

"It's important that I am the right 'fit' for your organization."

"I do have some commitments to honor, but yes, I *can* start next week."

What has *actually* gone through my mind while using the above phrases during interviews that are going badly includes:

"Yes, I'm a team player, but hopefully not on a team where everyone is as stiff as *you* are!"

"I don't mind traveling, as long as I stay at a nice hotel, and I don't have to do it more than four times a year."

"I think that I would have to be a combination of Superman and Henry Kissinger to 'fit' in your organization, based upon the job description."

"I currently have *nothing* going on, but I'm certainly not going to act as though I could start here this afternoon."

Take any interview offered. And even if, as a friend of mine from Georgia once said, "you have about as much chance of winning as a one-legged man in an ass-kicking contest," you really have nothing to lose from the experience.

# 26.

## CONSULTING

An acquaintance of mine (acquaintance is defined as someone who only calls you when they want something, a friend calls you just to talk) that left the employ of the same company as me took a job with a company owned by his next-door neighbor. Unfortunately, the new job fizzled after six months, and he found himself suddenly unemployed. I bumped into him after this occurred, and during the course of our conversation (I was still employed at this point) I said, "What are you doing now?" He replied rather airily, "I'm doing some consulting."

I find that "consulting" generally means "I'm unemployed" and using the term consultant to describe your current state of employment lets the informed world know that you still have your pride. There are any number of successful consultants in the world and an even larger number of unsuccessful ones. Using the title without giving any additional information provides you with an air of mystery to the uninformed, and to make an even bolder statement, you can have business cards made that state your name and title.

Having a business card made with a self-appointed title, such as consultant (or better yet, 'president' of your own consulting firm), gives you greater acceptability in a world that, seemingly, thrives on titles. The really great part about having business cards made with personal titles is that it is perfectly legal in all fifty states and cannot be contested in a court of law (unless you take a bunch of money for "consulting" and really screw someone's business up big time).

# 27.

## REAL ESTATE

Many people who have become unemployed from professional positions immediately look about for "something" that they can do that will provide the kind of income to which they are accustomed, without making a big career commitment, because they will go back to nearly any job that was as good as the one they just lost. Unfortunately for many, the sale of real estate appears on the horizon as the salvation to all economic woes. Gee, you take a couple of weekend courses, take an examination, and bingo—you are now a bona-fide real estate sales professional! This is true in most states except for California, where there are so many people with real estate licenses that I think they automatically give you one when you apply for a driver's license.

Prior to joining the corporation that suddenly unemployed me, I did a variety of things, which included a year's stint as a real estate salesman (hey, I was young and single at the time). What started out as a seemingly amusing way to make money degenerated, along with available business due to an alarming rise in mortgage interest rates, into a grim daily grind of sitting in an office making 'cold calls' and praying for the phone to ring with a possible buyer. Needless to say, after a year of *that* I was happy to take a position as a magazine editor for a small-trade journal that paid a lousy salary, but a salary nonetheless.

Over the years I maintained my license on the off-chance that I could supplement my income by the occasional sale of some real estate. I really kept it active so that I could hang out with one of the most erudite individuals I have ever known, who also happened to be a successful real estate broker. When I became suddenly unemployed, I nearly jumped at the opportunity to go back to selling real estate full time—as egregious an error as I made the first time around.

If you are considering real estate sales as an option when you find yourself unemployed, take a hard look at the newspaper. Scanning the real estate section of any newspaper will reveal photos of lots of cheerful people with snappy messages regarding the properties that they are offering for sale. Careful examination will reveal about a half dozen or so who are really making the big bucks. The rest of the people are probably just making ends meet, or have spouses with good jobs and full benefits.

The really successful people in real estate have all the warmth of a great white shark and can put most attorneys to shame when it comes to joining the feeding frenzy that the prospect of obtaining money engenders. Unless you are willing to swim with the sharks, avoid real estate at all costs.

# 28.
## READING

This is essential to the freshly unemployed, as well to everyone else, in my opinion. When you are employed, reading often means reviewing reports, staring at a computer screen, studying agendas, and mentally correcting the errors of others. When you become unemployed, you suddenly have some *time* to read what you *like*. This includes books, magazines, newspapers, cereal boxes, billboards, and nearly anything that requires you to cease "doing" and start "absorbing."

I have, thanks to my mother, been a prodigious reader all of my life. It's one of those things that come easily to me. Like baseball to a kid who has a natural affinity for the game, reading is a kind of addiction for me. It is very nearly impossible for me to sit on a toilet and not read something (I admit, I have been reduced to studying the chemical ingredients of shampoo on occasion.) I would read in my sleep if I could.

The suddenly unemployed have a golden opportunity to sit down and read anything that they want. Why? Because someone has made it *their* time to do what they want, when they want to do it! Even people who only read a novel once a year on the beach during their summer vacation are now able to read several chapters a day if they want to. It's a great time to get a library card (It's FREE—an important word at this point in your life) and peruse the stacks of your local library for what interests you, and not to feel as though you have to read what someone has sent you in the interoffice mail.

Reading provides a variety of avenues for the suddenly unemployed to travel upon, escape (you *need* this at this point in your life), information, self-improvement, humor, and a number of other self-indulgent directions. It's funny how certain books and articles stick with you long after they have passed beneath your gaze. When I was a kid, albeit an odd one (I think that now I would be classified as a "nerd"), I read some stuff that was definitely *not* on the hit list of my peers. I remember laughing out loud while reading Budd Schulberg's *Rally Round the Flag Boys*, and being amused and amazed at the wit and cleverness found in nearly anything written by Jack Douglas.

It's important to try to hit a balance in your reading as a suddenly unemployed individual. Too much escapism is like watching too much television, and not enough *Time* or *Newsweek* or *Money*—while relying solely on the daily newspaper—only gives you part of the story. It is okay to read some of the less-than-critical stuff. We receive two weekly *Shoppers*, which I read cover to cover (including the classifieds) to keep up on local events—besides, their contents are more interesting than the chemical ingredients of shampoo.

# 29.

## SOMETHING FOR NOTHING

As an eternal optimist, my thinking is often tempered by my wife's sage advice, "If it sounds too good to be true, it probably is." Undeterred by those words, I usually go forward, smiling, on yet another wild-goose chase. I naively tend to think that nearly everyone else in the world that seems to be friendly and outgoing is doing it in an altruistic sense. I am often reminded of, again, my wife's words when we were negotiating for an automobile about ten years ago. I had struck up a snappy conversation with the salesman and was discussing a variety of things with him when he received a phone call. When he took the call, my lovely bride leaned over and *sotto voce* said, "Rick, this guy doesn't want to be your *friend*, he wants to sell you a *car!*"

Recently, I heard on the radio that a "free (this is the first hint of disaster) career opportunity seminar for marketing consultants" was being held at a nearby hotel the following week. The radio message went on to say that "applicants" for these positions would receive a free laptop computer and qualify for car leases and various bonus plans. Needless to say, I couldn't resist.

One of the luxuries of being suddenly unemployed is having the time to pursue all possible job opportunities. Instead of furiously sending out resumes, it sometimes is worthwhile to do a little "field work" and attend things like job fairs and career seminars to round out your job-search experience. During my state of enforced vocational respite I attended various job fairs (these are opportunities to get free food and drink, sometimes, while company employees scrutinize you and your resume and smile so much that their cheeks must hurt for days afterward) and career seminars.

The "free laptop" career seminar was just too good to pass up, so I went. After registering via telephone, where they gave me a special reservation number (which, strangely, was not required when I showed up), I wrote the date on my calendar and planned that day around the big event. Two hundred intrepid souls were herded into a ballroom and introduced to the president of the company, who had made the trip from Dallas because "he felt that this was just too important a meeting to entrust anyone else in his company." After assuring everyone that this was *not* some type of come-on where he would be asking us to get out our checkbooks or credit cards, he informed us that his presentation would take approximately two hours of our "valuable" time (looking around, I saw a lot of retired-looking people, college student-age people, and unemployed-looking schmucks like myself).

This guy was *really* good. He oozed sincerity and personal success. He told us about how he began with nothing and was now a multimillionaire at the age of thirty-three (damn, I was in *high school* when this guy was born) with an eight thousand square foot home, five kids with their college tuition already paid for, and a garage full of exotic cars. He let everyone in the room know that he wanted to "share" his success with people having the "vision" to become successful entrepreneurs (uh-oh!). He continued on with this powerful message for nearly two hours before we got the first indicator that we were expected to part with some money. "By handing out these interactive CDs to prospects, you can expect a return far exceeding their $4.00 cost." The crowd hunched forward in anticipation, waiting for the inevitable.

Our speaker didn't disappoint. After reiterating the vast amounts of money we could make with his program, he, in salesman's parlance, "asked for the order." For the sum of only *twelve thousand dollars* we could join him on this incredible journey to personal wealth and success, which included a "free" laptop computer and "qualified" us for car leases and various bonus plans. What a deal!

I passed on this one.

# 30.
## AN OCCUPATIONAL BIOGRAPHY

As a reader, I am always fascinated to find out what I can from the flyleaf biography of an author. One of the most memorable is that of Louis L'Amour, a prodigious writer and impeccable researcher. Although his books are often viewed as something that Joe Average might pick up if he was looking for a good western to read, they exhibit excellent research and provide a true feeling of what the West was like. Mr. L'Amour's capsule biography, which accompanied most of his books, has always been my favorite:

*Louis L'Amour is a frontiersman by heritage (his grandfather was scalped by the Sioux) and a universal man by experience. Since leaving his native North Dakota, he's been, among other things, a longshoreman, lumberjack, elephant handler, and hay shocker. He's circled the world on a freighter, sailed a dhow down the Red Sea, been shipwrecked in the West Indies, been stranded in the Mojave Desert. As a professional boxer, he won 51 of 59 fights (three were draws). He has written more than 400 short stories and over 50 books.*

*He lives in Los Angeles with his wife Kathy, and their two children.*

Wow!

Keeping this kind of a biography in mind, perhaps it might be better to offer a prospective employer an occupational biography rather than the standard (and usually pretty stiff) resume.

I pondered (again) my past and decided to give it a try:

*Rick Dapp is a business-oriented guy by heritage (his father, grandfather, and great-grandfather were all in the insurance business) and a sort of universal man by experience. He has managed to graduate from the University of South Carolina, lived in four different states, and has been, among other things, a professional horseman, real estate agent, summer camp employee, magazine editor, freelance writer, employee of a Fortune 200 company, business consultant, technical writer, business analyst, frustrated musician, devoted husband, and father to two wonderful children. He has traveled to every state east of the Mississippi River, some of the ones west of there, Mexico, Canada, Aruba, the Bahamas, and Bermuda. He lives in eastern Pennsylvania with his wife Tris.*

Somehow, it's just not L'Amour, but it *is* more interesting than my resume.

# 31.

## PERCEPTIONS

As a child of the sixties and young man of the seventies, I embraced the age with a firm grip and tried my best to see how much shorter I could manage to make my allotted span. I managed to go through a variety of used English sports cars, motorcycles, chambray work shirts, and dingo boots. I also managed to grow a crop of hair, developed a lifelong fondness for delta blues, and managed to not get drafted. It was a lovely time to be alive.

Time marched on, and I eventually became part of the establishment that I attempted to deny by becoming employed, first as an editor of a small weekly trade journal, and then as an employee of a large corporation. Marriage and financial security became prime motivators in my metamorphosis. Often, when in the company of similarly-raised young(ish) professionals, the past would become alive—if only in our collective memories.

Recently, I found myself standing next to a young guy (I am at the stage in life when someone who is thirty seems young) who caused me to stare. He had a shaved head, double earrings in *both* ears, a beard, a tank top with a BMW motorcycle logo, and tattoos that began at his wrists and covered both arms entirely to the shoulders. My initial thought was, "Where on earth did *this* guy come from?" and assumed (a bad, bad thing to do) that he was probably a biker with a tenth-grade education and felony arrests in his background.

It hit me like a thunderclap: I was making assumptions about someone I didn't know a THING about. He noticed me looking at the tattoos, which really were art—with a number of Japanese word characters interspersed within them—and locked into my stare. I broke away visually and cautiously spoke; trying to remember what it was like to be a much younger man, "You ride?"

He grinned, actually grinned in a friendly manner, and said, "I ride all year round!" Given the fact that I live in Pennsylvania, this is a major accomplishment. I generally cease enjoying my aged Honda when the temperature drops below fifty degrees. He continued the conversation, telling me about the various vintage BMW motorcycles that he owned, as well as the Russian Ural bike that he used for winter motoring. Further inquiry revealed that he was a third-year student at Penn State, having served five years in the U.S. Navy (hence the tattoos and Japanese ideograms), and planned on a career as a teacher of English Literature on the college level.

I suppose the moral of this particular tale, if there is one, is that our perceptions allow themselves to be shaped by our experience. And if becoming suddenly unemployed was the catalyst that allowed me to regain control of my perception, it was worth the blow to the ego. I have made a conscious effort to shape my perception on *my* terms, and not upon those imposed upon me by an employer. No matter what occurs in the future, I will fight making assumptions about anything—or anybody, for that matter —without examining my motives. Becoming suddenly unemployed can free you of those restrictions.

# 32.

## NECK TIES

I have a collection of nice, silk neck ties, which represent a reasonably significant initial cash outlay, but I don't wear them anymore. Well, that's not entirely true; I *do* wear them when I go on job interviews. A tie says to a prospective employer that you are willing to be steady, conservative, mature, and incredibly boring if the need arises.

Ties used to be required before "business casual" became fashionable. I remember when it started with "casual Fridays" and then became "full-time business casual" at the corporation for which I toiled. It always seemed amusing to have a dress code enforced upon the white-collar employees when the folks working in the manufacturing facilities were able to wear whatever was comfortable. I always felt a little condescending when I visited a manufacturing plant in my conservative (dark) suit, solid color (blue or white) oxford cloth shirt, silk tie, and polished shoes. I was a "suit" to those people who were actually *making* something other than reports and marketing studies.

When you become suddenly unemployed, you have the opportunity to go from "full-time business casual" to "full-time unemployed comfortable." Just don't let yourself go from "full-time unemployed comfortable" to "chronically unemployed sloppy."

Keep a couple of ties in the closet. Sometimes you can fool people by walking upright and looking like the steady, conservative, mature type that you no longer are.

# 33.

## FAMOUS UNEMPLOYED PEOPLE I HAVE MET

The average person has limited personal exposure to famous people. We are inundated with them via the media, but really can't say that we have direct communication with them. Sure, you can watch the stars of sitcoms yuk it up in interviews on TV, or learn of their supposed personal traumas on the covers of supermarket tabloids (I sometimes pick one of those rags up and leaf through it while waiting for the person in front of me to unload an enormous cartload of groceries onto the conveyor—the story inside never seems to be as interesting as the headline on the cover), but you can't say that you *really* know them. One of my all-time-favorite books on this subject is *Famous People I Have Known* by Ed McClanahan —a kindred soul if there ever was one.

At first, I was willing to say that I have never had a conversation with a "famous" person, but after considering it for a while, I realized that I had. In my lifetime I have shaken hands and conversed with not one, but *two* famous people. And, get this, they were BOTH unemployed at the time!

The first unemployed famous person I ever met was former president Dwight D. Eisenhower. I was about twelve years old, and my father had managed to arrange for our family to go to his office at his farm in Gettysburg, Pennsylvania. It didn't sink in at the time that I was standing in front of the former leader of the free world and one of the greatest military leaders of the twentieth century. He was just a real friendly, older gentleman who kind of reminded you of somebody's grandfather. He was, of course, unemployed—having left office in 1960 to spend his remaining years at the farm. My kind of guy. It's too bad that I couldn't know that we'd have something in common later in my life. Perhaps he could have given me some advice.

The other famous person I met was Linda Blair, the child star of *The Exorcist*, who peaked pretty early in life and received a not-uncommon type of unemployment suffered by actors who become identified with a single, popular role. I was at a horse show in Tampa, Florida, a number of years ago, and some of the folks I knew were all gathered around an attractive, quiet girl in the stable area. One of the other girls told me to come over and meet the object of their animation. Unbeknownst to me, Linda Blair was an equestrienne of some accomplishment and was showing a horse at the week-long event. Obliging, I walked over and was introduced to the girl who gave head-twisting and vomiting a new dimension on the silver screen. I smiled and chatted with her, and when asked what I thought about her role in the movie, I had to answer honestly that I hadn't seen the picture (I still haven't!). Ms. Blair seemed amused by the answer and by my failure to be impressed—hell, she *was* technically unemployed at the time.

Politicians are great subjects for sudden unemployment, as are actors, most Olympic athletes, club musicians (weekly), overweight jockeys, and Tim Conway as a television sitcom star.

# 34.

## LOBBYING

Lobbying is one of those terms originally applied to those denizens in thousand-dollar suits who haunt the halls of Congress seeking favor for special interests. It has, probably due to the media, managed to become a term relative to anyone seeking support for their cause or personal agenda.

Suddenly unemployed people have a predilection for lobbying. It's one of those ploys to gain sympathy for their fate, and I'm as guilty as anyone. I can't begin to imagine how many times I have given a blow-by-blow description of how I was cast to the wolves by my former employer. It would be okay if I had been a political prisoner, or the subject of the McCarthy hearings in the 1950s, but, in retrospect, it's really whining for sympathy from anyone polite enough to listen.

People lobby all the time and without really thinking about it, either. Not long ago I was standing in a relatively long line to buy movie tickets, when a couple of kids ducked in ahead to join their already waiting friends. The woman in front of me turned, *to me*, and hissed, "Did you

SEE what those kids just did? As if this line wasn't long enough already!"

I nodded sagely and didn't say anything, but my mind was racing. Why was this woman addressing me with her problem? Why didn't she yell at the kids who were causing her anguish? Hell, everyone behind them in line had suffered the same fate. I guess it's a comment on the human condition when a total stranger, and someone whom you will probably never see again in your life, lobbies *you* to their cause.

I don't think I'm going to tell anyone else about my last day of corporate employment unless they specifically ask for the details.

# 35.

## SELF-HELP BOOKS

There is a household correlation between ownership of self-help books and personal exercise equipment. For every stationary bicycle (fairly expensive, but you can get one for free from your parents) gathering dust in the family room, there are at least five self-help books yellowing in a copier paper box in the attic. For every rowing machine (rarer, and more expensive), there are at least ten self-help books. And for every alpine ski machine (real expensive—for the amount of good it will do you), there is an entire shelf of self-help books somewhere in the house.

We are a nation of well-intentioned souls willing to part with money to make ourselves think that we will actually follow through with our desire to improve our looks and lifestyle. Callous? Maybe. Heck, *this* is a self-help book that, hopefully, a few people will read and appreciate.

How many of us actually make the shift from our ingrained habits and create sweeping changes in our lives? I have read books on time management, fitness, personal finance, personal relationships, and music appreciation. And, yes, I have owned a stationary bicycle and an alpine skiing machine. I never got around to acquiring a rowing machine, although I really wanted one for a while. I watch countless ads on television that espouse weight reduction plans, abdomen tightening machines, and personal care products. The plan is constantly presented to us but the motivation is often lacking—particularly when you are suddenly unemployed.

Being unemployed should provide the time to really get cracking on personal improvement. Unfortunately, nearly all of these plans require an investment of time *and* money. I see aging television stars and sports figures hawking exercise equipment and deals on gym memberships with one primary goal—getting you to part with your money so that you can look as good as they do. It's a dilemma for us unemployed folks whose income has been reduced to subsistence levels. We want to improve ourselves to make us more salable, but we can't afford the fee required.

Perhaps we need to establish a federal program aimed at personal improvement. We have had a former candidate for the presidency of the United States willing to promote a drug to cure erectile dysfunction. Why can't we have a federal agency whose sole function is to promote self-improvement?

# 36.

## KEEPING CURRENT

When you become unemployed, you are suddenly removed from the loop in which you existed, whether it was for six months or for thirty years. Being forcibly removed from an existence that you understood, and with which you were probably competent, means that you no longer have the daily dose of input that allowed you to remain at the top of your professional or technical form. You have suddenly not only become unemployed, you are probably no longer "current."

If you are a stockbroker, or a welder, or a social worker, or a chef, being "current" is important. It is more critical for the stockbroker to adopt this position than a welder because of the nature of their business. (Although, welders have to keep up on the latest technology in their trade if they are to command top-wage dollars, and they are more likely to find a job sooner than an unemployed stockbroker!) If you are separated from a job that didn't have a specific professional calling, such as engineering or accounting, you are more likely to fall off of the being-current merry-go-round than someone who has a set of professional credentials.

This failure to remain current was brought home to me recently in, of all things, an automobile. My faithful Isuzu, which has taken us close to two hundred thousand miles in ten years, developed an oil leak. Not just a couple of drops on the garage floor, but rather something akin to arterial bleeding. Needless to say, it had to go to the garage for evaluation and correction (it was a broken hose from the engine to the oil cooler for any motorheads that may be reading this). The unavailability of a part for the better portion of a week necessitated the loan of my mother-in-law's four-year-old Buick.

Now, when you spend most of a decade riding in what is essentially a four-wheel-drive truck with a roof rack and a back seat, driving an example of Detroit's most popular car for the over-sixty crowd is kind of unnerving. There is little road noise, everything in the car works, there are all sorts of little buttons to push, which are aimed at improving your comfort, and the transmission doesn't whine when you drive in reverse. I felt downright *retired* sitting in the leather seats with the climate control constantly adjusting to my desired degree of comfort.

I made a left turn on a hill approaching the road to my house and, as I proceeded up the hill, I began to hear a "bonging" noise over the sound of the radio (it was Deep Purple's "Highway Star" for any audiophile that may be reading this). Mildly alarmed at the alert, I thought that perhaps I had a door unsecured, until I looked at the dashboard and noticed that the left turn signal was still on. Somewhere in the past decade a designer had come up with a way to notify drivers too dense to remember to turn off the turn signal that it was time to push the little lever into the neutral position! I realized that I was no longer "current" in an automotive sense.

It may be a good time, if you are suddenly unemployed, to become more current by attending seminars, enrolling in a course offered by a local college, or reading up on your area of interest or expertise. It is deceptively easy to fall into the trap of believing what you *were* doing was "cutting edge," even though, in fact, you yourself was the edge that was cut.

# 37.
## FOCUS

One of the most perplexing things that occur to the freshly unemployed, at least to this member of the tribe, is the amazing amount of time that can be consumed in a day with no reasonable explanation as to how it was used. This becomes an especially thorny issue when a wife, husband, partner, or significant other—who *is* employed—comes home and says, "What did you do today?"

The problem here is focus. When you toil for a corporation, it's not hard to maintain focus. You have a schedule, a boss, a desk, and a reason for being exactly where you are at any given time during the day. It's easy to remain focused on your task. When you join the ranks of the suddenly unemployed, it can be akin to a ship—or a dinghy, depending upon your situation—that has suddenly had its rudder removed. You can get up in the morning with a variety of tasks in mind and face them with steely resolve, only to find yourself wondering what you accomplished at the end of your "working" day.

I have a friend who left the military to become a member of the production staff of a medium-sized, daily newspaper. He toiled there for ten years before he decided it was time to go into business for himself—with a dog kennel. After five years living with the dogs, and going a variety of directions with assorted financially questionable ventures, as well as working as a security guard and a bank courier to make ends meet, he regained his focus. He got a job as a car salesman for a local dealership and is now the manager of commercial truck accounts. It took him a while to realize that he needed a structured, hierarchical (military?) environment, where he could focus his energies and not be distracted.

I find that I cannot function without a list. I did this when I worked for a corporation, and I do it now. I write down *everything* I plan to do in a day's time—even things as trivial as replacing the light bulb in the front porch light. In the "straight" working world, I used a daily planner in a leather bound binder (with my initials on it). In the suddenly unemployed world, I use a spiral notebook, which is far less expensive than buying those page inserts punched with seven holes (why can't those people use three holes like the rest of the world?). I also write down my tasks in pen—no cheating with a number two pencil and an eraser—and stroke through each as it is completed. For folks obsessed with using electronic devices for this exercise, there are any number of computer programs and hand-held devices that allow you to generate lists. Unfortunately, it's also extremely easy to delete tasks with a keystroke rather than facing the permanence of ink.

This technique serves two purposes. It gives you an agenda for your "working" day, and, if you have a spouse or partner, provides a kind of "evidence" that you really *did* get something accomplished while they were on the job somewhere else. I always leave my evidence on the kitchen counter so that my wife can see it when she gets home.

It really does avoid the question of "what did you do today?"

# 38.

# WHAT'S FOR DINNER?

When you have two people working outside of the home, this question is often moot. "What's for dinner?" is usually a joint venture that, in our house, has been addressed by such things as spaghetti (easy), the ever-popular crock pot (also easy, but often boring), frozen pizza (*real* easy—and a big hit with the kids!), and the ever-present leftovers.

In keeping with the regimen of a daily agenda, preparing dinner is a staple item on each page of *my* spiral notebook. For the suddenly unemployed, planning the most important family event of the day can be both challenging and gratifying (God, don't let me sound like Martha Stewart). Well, it *can* be, and there are some rules:

1. Never duplicate the same meal during any given week, your spouse and children will notice.
2. Never ask your kids what they would like for dinner, because the answer is always "McDonalds!"
3. Never try to convince your family that "surf and turf" is a combination of Mrs. Paul's fish sticks and hot dogs.

4. When trying out anything spicy on your family, always have some sort of bland alternative warming in the oven (either becomes leftovers if not used that day).

5. Avoid asking your spouse/partner/significant other to "pick something up on the way home" unless you have a *real good* reason (like nuclear attack, invasion by aliens, tsunami). However, if they offer to "pick something up" on the way home, accept eagerly and gratefully.

6. Never, ever, have nothing planned for dinner and expect to be able to say, "I was just *too* busy to get something together for dinner," without serious repercussions. Even the most impressive task list lying on the kitchen counter cannot overcome this error in judgment.

# 39.

## PEOPLE WHO CAN'T HELP YOU TO GET A JOB

There are any number of people in the world of the suddenly unemployed person who have absolutely no ability to find a job for that person. But that's okay.

It is important to keep in touch with people who shared your work experience, benefited from your expertise, were customers, or were simply willing listeners before you joined the tribe. Most of them can do *nothing* in terms of offering you gainful employment.

On the wall above my desk (why, I'm looking at it right now) is a framed certificate that was created by an artist and illustrator who worked with me in the same department for five or six years. It is entitled "The Humane Award of the Month" and was "presented" to me in my role as "Possum Man" while a member of the department. It was a gag that this gentleman put together after I noticed an opossum stranded on the median of the interstate highway, which ran right past the building in which we were located. I managed to involve not only the local humane society, but the Pennsylvania State Police as well, when they shut down a lane of traffic so that the opossum could be rescued.

A year or so after this little escapade, my friend the artist was diagnosed with a cancerous tumor and had a fairly delicate operation which, fortunately, was successful but left him somewhat impaired physically. I dropped in to see him the day after the surgery, and then spent a lunch hour with him a couple of days later. It's just one of those things you do for a friend, isn't it?

As it turned out, I was one of the very few who *did* go to visit this guy at the hospital (even our *boss* didn't bother to check in personally). And ever since then, every time I am in the company of this gentleman (who was forced into early retirement by "our" company), he reminds me of my kindness in visiting him while he was in the hospital.

Another person who won't hire me is now the president of his own electronics firm and the employer of over fifty people. When I first met him, he was working for another company as the general manager. He subsequently left to start his own company and, as he began to seek business, approached me about obtaining certification as a vendor for the very large company for which I worked (the very same one that made me suddenly unemployed—imagine that). I went to work on the corporate purchasing division and managed to step on enough of their turf that the head of purchasing called me and chastised me for interceding. Fortunately, the purchasing department minions felt that the start-up electronics company possessed the qualities necessary to be awarded vendor status and granted it. To this day, I can call this growing company and be immediately passed on to the office of the president, who periodically reminds me of my involvement in winning the battle with the purchasing department.

It is very important for the suddenly unemployed to maintain contact with people for whom nice things have been done, who cannot—or will not—offer you a job. They make really terrific references on your resume.

# 40.

## FALSE STARTS

While having lunch with a friend, who happens to be an extremely successful stockbroker, the subject of my employment quest came up. After regaling him with various adventures in temporary employment, he looked at me and said, "What is it that you *really* want to do?"

A stunning question! The simplicity of it walloped me right between the eyes. Having been rejected so many times, I had reached the point where I had lowered my expectations to a point at which I would have taken nearly anything that offered a reasonable salary and benefits. This question, from a guy who also figured largely in the string of rejections (he had arranged an interview with his brokerage house and, after taking the aptitude test, I was told by the general manager that I didn't have the killer instinct to become a really successful broker), made me realize that I had strayed from the path of satisfying employment. I thought for a moment, while chewing a mouthful of Reuben sandwich, swallowed (my mom trained me well), and said, "publishing."

Having been an editor of a trade journal twenty years previously developed a true love for the business of publishing. The only reason I left the magazine's employ was the need for a living wage. I had worked in an office on the second floor of a large printing company with two web presses and a multitude of Miller and Crabtree sheet-fed presses. It was a great place to work, with six magazines and a book publisher all located above the din of the ground floor operations.

Armed with my most-recent revelation, I bade farewell to my friend and headed home for the phone and the trusty yellow pages. Perusing the publishers available in my area, I began cold calling everyone in the phone book. The pitch was that I was trying to assess the opportunities in publishing and wondered if the publisher could spare me fifteen minutes to discuss it. Not surprisingly, a number of them said that they either weren't hiring, didn't have the time, or could spare me the time if I could keep it to the requested amount because they were *very* busy.

One of the firms that granted me access was a publisher of magazines and books geared to the special interest crowd. Arriving five minutes early (my dad trained me well, saying once that it was "critical to be no more than ten minutes early, nor more than two minutes late for an appointment"), I waited fifteen minutes while the woman who had granted me the interview finished a phone call. Upon entering her office and making the obligatory observations of how nicely the office was furnished, I checked my watch. We discussed my past while she scanned my resume and discovered that we had both worked for the same publishing company twenty years previously. She arrived there only weeks after my departure and was familiar with "my" magazine. This was looking very good indeed!

She told me that they had no editorial positions available but did have an opening for an advertising manager for two of their titles. I checked my watch, noted that my fifteen minutes were up, and asked if we could schedule an interview for the advertising position. Incredibly, she said yes, and we set a date. The second interview, primarily a formality, resulted in a job offer and a description of the salary and commission schedule. I was in!

Starting on the first day of May, I found myself back in the wonderful world of publishing with a company populated with neat people who actually liked their jobs and accepted me as an advertising manager. After the first week in this euphoria, I found myself singing in the car on the way to work and thinking that I couldn't believe that they were actually *paying* me to work there. It was a great feeling, one that I hadn't had for a long, long time.

At eight thirty on Monday of the third week, a message popped up on the screen of my computer telling everyone that there would be a staff meeting at ten o'clock in the conference room. I thought that this was probably normal, since it was the beginning of the week, and that we would all get an inspiring call to greater excellence in our endeavor. I couldn't have been more wrong.

The publisher began the meeting with a revelation: "The company has been for sale since last December, and although we had a bona fide buyer, a financial crisis has caused him to back out of the agreement. As of end of business today, we are closing the doors, and all employees will be released."

I looked around the room at the expressions of stunned disbelief and thought, "Gee, *here's* a familiar feeling." As the question-and-answer period ensued, I sat with a sense of detachment and, surprisingly, found myself watching reactions to the news by coworkers. They ranged from sobbing to stony silence, and I realized that the only people in the room who were handling it well were the ones who had been terminated before.

I was a veteran, and I could handle it—again.

# 41.

## WHERE ARE THEY NOW?

When you are unemployed, you watch a lot of television. Actually, you don't necessarily watch it as much as you have it turned on for company during the day. The simple existence of the medium makes me wonder about people who shine brightly and briefly on the screen and then, as abruptly, disappear. Some of them reappear consistently on other programs, but some never seem to return to the zenith of television fame. My apologies to persons who have died or are otherwise inconvenienced notwithstanding, but where *are* some of these people?

Admittedly, Tom Hanks has done well for himself, but where is that other guy who starred with him on *Bosom Buddies*? And where is Michael Parks—the star of *Then Came Bronson*? Speaking of Bronsons, where are Charles and the other one, Pinchot? Whatever became of Tommy Kirk, Ahna Capri, and Bobby Goldsboro? And does Bobby still have that awful hairdo? Where is Will Hutchins—remember *Sugarfoot*? And where the heck is the entire cast of *The High Chaparral*? I want to know.

I suppose, to borrow a phrase from the practice of public relations, it's a matter of *positioning* in your field of endeavor. Since the inception of this book, I learned that Charles Bronson, a fine actor and great individualist, died following a lengthy illness. The other folks became so well-known in the characters that they played, that it probably became difficult to find fame again due to their past roles. When looking for a job, you need to decide if you want the same thing—again—or if you want to position yourself in a new role. Take a hard look at what you are and what you want to be before striking out on the road to re-employment.

# 42.

## MOLDING YOUNG MINDS

During a party (yes, you may go to parties when you are unemployed) a neighbor asked "the question." If you are not unemployed, you have no conception of the slight halt in pulmonary function that accompanies "the question." Only people who are unemployed, especially those who have been unemployed for some time and have become fully sensitized, can appreciate this.

"What are you doing these days?" she asked brightly.

Unless you have rehearsed a stock answer to this (and even if you have, and it is asked when you are unprepared), there is a brief pause required for the alarm to subside.

"Uhhh, I've been doing a number of things," I replied.

The word "consulting" leapt to mind, as did "part-time work," and "working for my brother-in-law." However, she had caught me at an unprepared moment, and I ended up with the generic, vague, non-answer to "the question."

"Well," she continued, "a good friend of mine has been substitute teaching and says that she can work as much, or as little, as she wants to."

Substitute teaching. Now *there's* one that I never considered. Just the term conjured up images of those nameless, unremembered people who stood in front of us in school and made a vague attempt at continuing our education in the absence of the regular teacher. The "subs" were usually retired teachers who filled in for the regular educator, primarily maintaining discipline in the classroom and little else. The only famous person I could remember admitting to being a substitute teacher was comedian-actor Robert Klein. He had a really funny routine that described some of his experiences "subbing" in New York City. Of course, *we* never had Robert Klein—or anyone even remotely resembling him—as a "sub" when we were in school.

My neighbor continued her discourse on how her friend obtained an (to me) unenviable position as a classroom dragon. Apparently, there was a critical need for substitutes in the area schools, and in Pennsylvania it was possible for anyone with a college degree to obtain an "emergency certification" for teaching. The emergency certification was issued after attending a two-day training session and then the certified substitute was allowed to participate in the educational process. After informing me that her friend was earning $100 a day to be a substitute, I began to see some possibilities forming. Gee, you started at eight o'clock and were done by three; you didn't have to correct homework or tests, and had a new answer to "the question."

I hastened to the regional district offices and presented myself for scrutiny. I had to obtain various reports from the state that certified that I was not a convicted felon or child molester, and filled out reams of forms. I then attended the obligatory two-day training session and, after sitting successfully through various presentations by teachers and administrators, I was given an emergency certification. Little did I know that I was also about to be thrown to the wolves.

Substitute teachers, to the unenlightened, are awakened by the telephone at five thirty in the morning and, upon answering (acting as if they were already up, showered, and dressed) are asked, "Are you available to substitute today?" This is almost as disarming as "the question." After receiving the assignment, the freshly minted substitute wakes up, showers, drinks the first of three cups of coffee, and madly looks about for an outfit suitable for education. Fortunately, schools have become more "office casual" in the dress code, and slacks and a nice shirt (tie optional) are acceptable. The unwitting substitute is told when to arrive and given the street address of the school, but is *not* told that there is virtually no parking within five blocks of the school.

Upon arriving breathlessly at the school office with minutes to spare, the substitute is given the class list, lunch list, and is told that the regular teacher has a "sub folder" on the desk. Given arcane directions to the location of the room, the substitute proceeds down the wrong hall, being given sidelong glances by the students at their lockers in the hall. Reaching the room, the substitute is greeted by a gathering of listless juveniles—each with a fully-loaded backpack—and a locked door. Any attempt at levity is greeted with blank stares by the students, and any inquiry regarding a key for the door is answered with a mass shoulder shrug. Suppressing a rising sense of panic, the substitute admonishes the gathered students to "just sit tight" (another round of blank stares and a group shrug) and returns to the office where the now-harried secretary shakes her head and says, "It was supposed to be unlocked. I'll have to get a custodian to unlock it for you."

Upon returning to the room, with custodian in tow, the fresh substitute (as in fresh meat) is greeted by a formerly compact herd of students now scattered throughout the hall, looking in the doors of neighboring classrooms, and noisily disrupting whatever educational endeavors attempted therein. The pandemonium is broken by a voice that sounds like sheet metal being forcibly torn in half (that any Marine Corps drill instructor would envy) with, "You kids all SHUT UP and get in a line against the lockers!" The origin of the voice is generally a small woman, demurely dressed, who probably drives a Saturn, and looks like she collects ceramic frogs. She looks pityingly at the substitute, glares at the students, shakes her head in antipathy, and returns to her classroom, slamming the door behind her. Now the real fun begins.

Students with a substitute teacher (especially an inexperienced one) before them in the classroom *never* all sit in their assigned seats, thereby making the seating chart useless. After fruitlessly attempting to take roll, the substitute sometimes searches vainly for the "sub folder" in the regular teacher's desk. After scanning all of the papers on the top of the desk, the substitute tries the desk drawers, only to find them locked. Looking pleadingly at the assembled class, the substitute is greeted by a mixture of looks, which include cunning, apathy, scorn, and, if he or she is *very* lucky, one kid (usually a girl) with a smile on their face.

Do not assume that the smiling student has your best interests at heart; even serial killers probably smile as they approach the next victim. However, the smiling student is probably the most likely candidate for assistance in obtaining information regarding the general direction of education in the classroom. This student is, if sincere, probably also sitting in her assigned seat and, therefore, has a name.

If you are very, very lucky the smiling student (let's call her Heather—you'll have at least three of them in any class) will tell you who is not in attendance that morning. However, by looking at the attendance list and not at the class, you have given the students an opportunity to begin to establish a pack mentality. If there are computers in the room, the students will gravitate toward them at this point, and unless you are very firm, they will fire them up and begin visiting websites that you never knew existed.

Incidentally, if subbing in inner-city schools, you will be exposed to class lists with names that you possibly have never seen before. Unfortunately, if you don't have a "Heather" to serve as your guide through attendance, you will have to attempt to pronounce them. If the list includes names like Shaniqua and I'Tasha, and you are unsure of the pronunciation, call out the last names. Some of the most irritated responses I have ever received have been from kids who have had their names mispronounced. Perhaps I'm showing my age, but no one ever seems to name their children Virginia, Ruth, Helen, Steve, Marlin, or Charlie any more.

Visits to the faculty room/lounge during the day are usually very enlightening experiences. Actually, the faculty "lounge" is generally a misnomer. It is quite often a room formerly used to store janitorial supplies, which now consists of a soda machine, a coffee pot (always empty), and several battered tables with similar folding metal chairs retired from the cafeteria years previously. A visit to the faculty room will allow the opportunity to overhear some truly classic observations by "real" educators.

"How are you getting along with Tyrone?" asked teacher #1.

"Not bad. Thanks for getting him transferred to *my* class!" said teacher #2, acidly.

"Have you heard the *mouth* on that kid?" asked teacher #3.

"Yeah. When I asked him about it, he told me he thought he had Tourettes Syndrome!" said teacher #2.

This isn't to say that all days spent in the classroom as a substitute are unrewarding. I've had episodes that renew my hope in childkind coming from unexpected quarters. Once, when I actually agreed to substitute in an elementary school, I arrived to find that the third grade class to which I was assigned would be traveling by bus on a field trip to an educational center about forty-five minutes away. I thought, "Wow, it's a *babysitting* day, and I won't have to keep the little darlings occupied all day."

Wrong.

After trying to round up all of the kids to put them on the bus (I mentioned to one of the other teachers that this exercise was akin to herding cats) and making sure that all of the bagged lunches had been placed in a cardboard box (I, of course, didn't have one), we rolled on to our destination. Arriving at the city where our field trip would be occurring, the bus driver admitted that she was lost and had no idea where the educational center was located. This required yours truly to exit the bus and begin asking people on the street where we were and how we could locate our destination. I know that real men aren't supposed to ask directions, but I had visions of riding around town with a busload of screaming third graders, so I left my pretensions on the bus and became a sidewalk supplicant. Fortunately, we found a nice lady who knew exactly where we were to go.

Arriving at the center, we all went through the various learning stations and presentations and later had lunch. I found a soda machine and satisfied my thirst with something carbonated. At this point, the kids discovered the gift shop and went wild trying to get rid of any money they had on a variety of stuff made in China. One of the boys approached me and engaged me in conversation.

"Mr. Dapp, are your gonna be our sub tomorrow?"

"I believe your regular teacher will be back tomorrow," I replied.

"Well, could you loan me a dollar, and the next time you're at our school I could pay you back?"

"Why do you need a dollar?" I said cautiously.

"There's a stethoscope in the gift shop for seven dollars, and I only have six."

I pondered the request as I reached into my pocket to fish out a dollar and thought, *If I never see this child again, all I've lost is a dollar, and, who knows, it may inspire him to become a doctor.*

Call me naive, but I'm a sucker for a sincere kid.

# 43.

## SAVING MONEY

When you are seriously unemployed, you become seriously interested in saving money, particularly after the unemployment checks stop. You begin turning unnecessary lights off, eliminating unnecessary car trips, discover that the store brands are still cheaper than national brands with coupons, and generally making your family miserable with your penury. You find that living in the dark, saying "no" to requests for trips to the convenience store for popsicles, and making everyone eat stuff that doesn't taste as good as the name brands, accounts for a savings of approximately eleven bucks over a month's time. However, there come moments when you can really assert yourself and announce a plan for saving some *real* money.

In my case, it was automotive.

It became apparent that one of our vehicles was suffering from "tired starter." This is a condition that becomes apparent when you turn the key and the starter just makes a clicking noise even though the battery is fully charged. My brother, the king of rolling junk when it came to cars (he continually purchased aged luxury cars that "just need a little detailing") showed me the temporary cure for "tired starter" with a hammer. When the starter clicks, you obtain a hammer and slide beneath the car, locate the starter (usually covered with grease and dirt and next to an exhaust pipe), and give it a solid whack. Often the car starts after this treatment, sometimes it doesn't.

Having been raised on a farm, I was reasonably knowledgeable in the workings of the internal combustion engine. And I was confident that I could address the starter problem after receiving an estimate of nearly three hundred dollars for a repair in a garage. I announced to the family that *I* would be repairing the starter in the confines of *our* garage at a great savings to us all. The plan was simple, remove the starter, have it rebuilt, and reinstall it. Piece of cake for an ol' farm boy like me.

I parked the car in our garage after the rest of the family left for school and work and began the process confidently. I had the tools, the knowledge, the time (I'm unemployed), and no clue as to how miserable this experience would become. American automobile manufacturers have, for some unknown reason, elected to place the starter in one of the most inaccessible places on the vehicle. Typically, it is located on the bottom side of the back of the engine behind an exhaust pipe where it becomes covered with black, oily dirt. It also requires contortionist abilities to get a wrench on the bolts holding it in place. Additionally, it requires skill of a Rubik's Cube master to get it out of the maze of engine gadgetry located around it. What seemed like an hour's work stretched into the early afternoon before I got the damn thing out of the car.

After taking the starter off to be rebuilt and picking it up again the following day, I was faced with the replacement procedure. Simply the reverse of the removal, right? Possibly, if you have the presence of mind to write down *exactly* how it came out of the bowels of the engine. Add to this the fact that, although the starter was clean and repainted from the rebuild shop, it became quickly covered with dirty engine grease and virtually impossible to hold while trying to line up the bolt holes and reinstalling the bolts. I was now into the third day of this simple job.

Finally, after using language that no member of my family has ever heard pass my lips, I thought I had it back in place, only to find that I had stripped the threads on one of the two bolts that hold it in place. Covered with black grease from fingertips to elbows and with aching shoulders from lying on a concrete floor, I called "uncle" and cautiously started the car, later driving it to a local garage where a mechanic repaired the stripped bolt threads and charged me eighty bucks for his time.

Doing some quick math, calculating the cost of the starter rebuild, the professional garage repair, and my time (based upon what I was making before I was suddenly unemployed), the cost of curing the tired starter problem came to nearly six hundred bucks. And I had black dirt etched into every crevice of my hands, which took nearly a week of scrubbing to eliminate.

I also promised my wife that I would write "I will not try to save money doing automotive repairs" one hundred times on a blackboard if that thought ever entered my mind again.

# 44.

## TRAVEL

If you are fortunate enough to have a spouse with a career that enables her—or him—to travel to far-flung places attending conferences, you may have the opportunity for travel that basically costs airfare and food. I am indeed fortunate to be married to a woman who periodically has to attend these events and is kind enough to share her hotel room with her husband and son. In the past, when I was employed, I often traveled to California and took them with me whenever possible. They went touring while I stood in the booth of a trade show, and we usually went to scenic locales together on the weekend before returning home.

Just because you are unemployed, doesn't mean that you have to be homebound when the opportunity to travel appears. Most schools will allow you to take your children along on these adventures if you can convince them that they are "educational" in nature (it was hard to justify two days at Disneyland in this regard, but I felt that riding Space Mountain was pretty educational for our son). Upon becoming unemployed, I despaired of traveling again, but my dear wife has managed to get us to Colorado, New

Orleans, San Francisco, Nashville, and other interesting places for the cost of airfare and food.

These trips not only expand everyone's horizons, but serve another valuable purpose. If you are contacted for a job interview, particularly one for which you have little interest, you can say truthfully, "Gee, I can't come in to see you next week because I'll be in Dallas all week. What does the following week look like for you?" The prospective employer may think that (1) you are going for a job interview, (2) your "consulting" job is taking you across the country, or (3) you don't really *need* their job and may reconsider the misanthropic salary offer they were considering when you did come for the interview. The key in this strategy is to *not* tell them *why* you are going. Keep them guessing—always.

# 45.

# IT'S NOT STATIC

One of the worst mistakes the unemployed person can make is to begin believing that things are not changing in the world around him or her. Once you are removed from the mainstream, floating in the quiet tributary of the discharged, there is a tendency to become focused on the immediate environment and detached from the larger world you previously enjoyed.

The existence of the unemployed person can be viewed as a small circle within at least two progressively larger circles. The small circle is your immediate, enforced, environment—home, family, close friends, and community. The next circle is the slightly larger one that includes your former employer (or employers), the geographical region in which you live (with prospective employers for whom you may want to work), and the places you frequented and the things you did when you were employed. The largest of the circles is the world as you know it.

Just because you have been removed from the daily grind, does not mean that you are removed from the turn of events as our planet completes its daily pirouette. The incessant sensory barrage of images and sound from television, radio, and the printed word keeps you aware of events and trends in the largest circle. A constant stream of information from your family and friends keeps you aware of changes within your immediate environment. It's that damn second circle that becomes the problem.

As time goes by, your early hopes for quick resolution of your employment dilemma are replaced by a cheerful outlook for prospects to improve. Then comes the quiet desperation of the long term. The second circle goes out of focus and periodically disappears from view altogether. As your prospects dim and the employment picture goes from colorful to monochromatic, it is only natural to retreat to the safety and comfort of your inner circle. Unless you are living alone with no electricity or neighbors while solidly within that inner circle, it is impossible to avoid knowing what is going on in the third, largest circle. Turn on the television for a healthy dose of audiovisual stimuli loaded with information about current happenings in the third circle. Unfortunately, there is a sad lack of available communication from that second circle. Occasionally, though, reports from the third circle will include messages from the second.

I received a message from the second circle via the third regarding a website for local and regional employment. It was an advertisement on the radio (I was in the car) with a catchy jingle, which included the web address. While steering the car with my knee and trying to avoid running into various mobile and immobile objects, I located a pen and a piece of paper from the console and jotted it down. Upon returning home, I fired up the computer (I was fired up, too) to access the website. While typing the web address, the little box on the screen first displayed, conveniently, a previously stored web address starting with the same letter. The displayed address was for an employment agency that I had approached over a year before, and I made a mental note to visit their site to see if any interesting jobs had been posted. Remember, I was *on fire* with visions of employment opportunities at this moment.

The local/regional employment website (with the catchy jingle) didn't have anything that seemed appropriate to my skill set. Incidentally, if you want to ensure your future employability, I have determined that you should become either a registered nurse or have something to do with information technology (really savvy college students take note—think *dual major*). So I keyed in the web address of the employment agency which, as it turns out, *did* have a job for which I was *eminently* suited. The woman who owned the agency was the only "personnel person" in my period of unemployment who actually seemed genuinely interested in finding me a job. The effort came to naught, but I retained warm feelings for her attempt.

I sent a nice e-mail to her, reminding her of our past relationship, and inquired about the job posting on their website. After hearing nothing from her in two days, I found myself driving within blocks of her office and thought that a personal call may force the issue. Arriving at the parking lot behind her building, I noticed her Saab convertible sitting on the other side and realized that, although she may not have time to see me, she would, at least, know that I cared enough too make a personal call and show my great interest in the available position. Walking past the Saab, I noticed that it was a little dirty and that the windows had a layer of dust on them, as if the car had not been used recently. Entering the office, I encountered a gentleman at the reception desk, and, upon simultaneously introducing myself and looking to see if my quarry was in her office, I said, "Is Patty in?" To which he replied somberly, "I'm sorry, but Patty passed away seven months ago."

As it turns out, the gentleman to whom I was speaking was her husband, who had taken over the daily operations of the office after retiring from another company. I offered sympathies and then mentioned that I had sent her an e-mail with a current resume and asked about a job posting. He replied that he "hadn't checked her e-mail messages for a couple of days," and he would "be in touch soon." I have yet to hear from him.

Reflecting upon the experience on the way home from Patty's office, I was struck by the fact that over a year had passed in my unemployment, and not only was I still unemployed—or, at least, underemployed—but someone from the second circle who had tried to help me had died, and I didn't have a clue.

If you are unemployed, live in the first circle, focus on the second, and be aware of the third. It's critical to your future success.

# 46.

## FUN THINGS TO DO ON SLOW DAYS

Certainly, you will have days when absolutely nothing worthwhile is happening in an employment sense. These are days when you need to allow your creative side to take over and to turn gloom into something a little brighter.

If, for example, you receive a call from a telemarketer, use the opportunity to shine a light not only on your existence, but to conduct a personal experiment in psychology.

Instead of listening for a few seconds and then saying, "Thanks, but I'm not interested," ask *them* questions. Remember, not only are these people taking up your time and intruding upon your home life, but they only have a limited amount of optimum time in which to do so. If the call comes at dinnertime (duh, what *other* time do these people seem to call?) try to see how long you can keep them on the line. Ask questions like, "Where do you live? Do you have children? What kind of car do you drive? Do you like macaroni and cheese? What is the first thing that comes to your mind when I say "festival?"

You'll be amazed at how these folks react to *you* prying into their lives and how much more enjoyable it is when you thank them for their time and then say, "Thanks, but I'm not interested."

Rather than dwelling upon your employment, or lack of, situation, you should move yourself, perhaps forcibly, to something completely removed from it. If gardening is an interest, and it's a windy, cold day in March, invest in some seed packets (inexpensive) and start growing seedlings for spring on a tray in the window on that sunny spot in the living room. Or, if you're feeling a little out of shape, unlimber that bicycle hanging in the garage and go for a ride (free) making sure to wave gaily to everyone you pass. With time on your hands and no active prospects for employment on the immediate horizon, you can volunteer at the local senior center (free, and personally gratifying), check out books you've been meaning to read at the local library (free), or simply go for a walk (free, and healthy).

Just because you're not making any money, doesn't mean you have to spend any to be perfectly happy.

# 47.
## A ROUND TUIT

A number of years ago there was a simple line drawing of a circle with the legend "A Round Tuit" and some sort of a moralizing story that went with it regarding procrastination. I can't recall the story, but I was reminded of the phrase recently as I was sifting through the daily mail.

The mail included the obligatory quantity of catalogs. My wife receives every catalog in America. I'm certain of it. And her name is on all the address labels. I am charged with disposing of the catalogs, and I constantly search for new and inventive ways of placing them anywhere but in the trash can. I found a dumpster in a nearby town that actually was designated for residents' magazines and catalogs, and would surreptitiously unload cartons of catalogs in it. Unfortunately, the town fathers must have figured out that there was a lot more recycling action in the dumpster than they expected, and it has been removed.

Anyway, I was perusing the mail, and one of the catalogs fell open to a page that showed a black baseball cap with the words "The Man, The Myth, The Legend" printed on it in white letters. I was instantly amused, because I have a good friend who, for some reason lost in the mists of time, began calling me "The Legend" when greeting me. I, of course, referred to him as "The Legend" upon seeing him or especially when introducing him to new people—it's a *guy* thing, and I wouldn't expect women to understand.

Looking at the picture of the baseball cap, I made a mental note to order it for him as a gift when I got around to it. And when I went to look for the catalog I (1) couldn't remember what company it was, (2) couldn't remember in which pile of catalogs it reposed, and (3) didn't dare ask my wife, because she would know that I, again, had procrastinated on something. As I sifted through seemingly hundreds of catalogs in copier-paper boxes in the garage, I realized that "getting around to it" had become a problem to this unemployed person. Since I had more time on my hands, I had allowed myself the luxury of putting things off until I was either good and ready or realized that I had to meet some sort of imposed deadline.

In the working world, I lived by the employer's schedule and by my own day timer. In the unemployed world, I began living by my own schedule and allowed the personal calendar to reside in locations where I had to find it to check appointments (kind of like that catalog with the baseball cap in it). In the working world, I had business obligations in which other people depended upon my contributions. In the unemployed world, I had this considerable amount of seemingly spare time in which I could do things at my own pace.

I found the catalog about two-thirds of the way through the catalog collection and immediately called the toll-free number to order it. "The Legend" enjoyed it enormously and now calls me "The Myth" in deference to my uncanny ability to locate objects that are appropriate to the circumstance. And after flipping through hundreds of pages of four-color photos of clothing, bedspreads, pecan logs, hard-to-find tools, backpacks, cheese, automobile accessories, luggage, candy, Santa Claus underwear, chunky costume jewelry, and more, more, more, I realized that I had an idea for my *own* catalog.

I will go through as many catalogs as possible and find as many abstruse items as I can, and then I'll contact suppliers willing to drop-ship this stuff based upon the enormous demand I will create. The title of my catalog, in bold letters across the cover, will be *Crap You Really Don't Need to Buy*. It will be revolutionary marketing in the catalog industry and will make millions.

I just know it will work, when I get around to it.

# 48.

## FOREVER YOUNG

There is a truly great song written by Bob Dylan, which was popularized by Rod Stewart, called "Forever Young" and has become an anthem for those of us who are growing older but refuse to grow up. As an unemployed adult, I have found that I have been forced to forgo the small pleasures of foolish humor in the workplace. The kind of activities that adults share to remind themselves that they still have the inner child, or inner teenager, in their psyche.

No longer can I conspire with coworkers to commit practical jokes or create pranks to relieve the tensions of "work." One that comes to mind had to do with putting the confetti from the office hole punch in a coworker's umbrella. The plan is to have the paper "dots" stored in the furled umbrella, so that when the unsuspecting owner pops the umbrella open at the door of the building prior to walking through the rain to the car, she or he is showered with paper. The evidence for the coconspirators is a scattering of confetti *everywhere* in the vicinity of the building entrance. Once, when we planned one of these events, a variable occurred that we hadn't planned on. Our boss, who was called unexpectedly to a meeting on a rainy day, asked to borrow a "loaded" umbrella from the intended prank victim. There was an air of disbelief and mild panic among those responsible as our exalted leader headed for the door. Fortunately, he had, like us, spent a number of years in the corporate trenches and was vastly amused that he had been pranked by his employees.

To retrieve the sense of being forever young as an unemployed adult, I discovered that spending as much time with the kids became a worthy alternative. When you are unemployed, you discover that your "free" time, in addition to being as remunerative as the title implies, allows you the luxury to become a coach, a mentor, a Cub Scout den leader, a transportation coordinator, a field trip chaperone, and a friend to kids who need an adult that they can trust. The upside to this (actually there is no downside) is that you become "one of the guys," and you find out about a variety of things that you would never have learned if you only had limited time to spend with kids. By simply showing up for little league baseball practices on a daily basis, you become an assistant coach by default. When you take your son to Cub Scout meetings —and stay—you become an assistant den leader.

I have found that because I am unemployed and have used my free time to help with kids' activities, I am more in tune with what is going on with the younger generation. I listen to conversations in the car and arguments on the playing field. I am allowed to share "kid humor," because I am trusted. I am used as a conduit to relay messages to adults and parents that would never have been sent or received otherwise. I know what is important to kids and what is dismissed as inconsequential.

As long as I stay in touch with these guys I will remain forever young.

# 49.

## WALK A MILE IN MY SHOES

A number of years ago, probably more than I'd like to admit, Joe South recorded a song called "Walk a Mile in My Shoes," which often comes to mind when I'm feeling sorry for myself as an unemployed (or underemployed) member of society. The song's ringing refrain filled my head as I took a four-day stint as a substitute teacher for a career-training class in an inner-city, "alternative" school. The "alternative" school is a recent development in our educational system that separates the discipline problems from the general student population and attempts to instill a little organization into their lives. The kids in this particular school refer to it as "jail," and all are generally unhappy to be there.

Having been brought up in a rural setting in the 1960s where the only time *anyone* was suspended from school was when a fistfight broke out among the jocks on school property. Being placed in an environment where several hundred souls are being monitored and disciplined on an ongoing basis was a real eye-opener for me. Had I not been downsized by corporate America, I never would have had the opportunity for exposure to the "alternative" environment. If

I were still in my undisturbed office billet, I would probably be making self-serving judgments about how very poorly our educational institutions are handling the needs of our kids.

This particular school is operated by a private corporation under contract to the school district and has a more pragmatic approach to education than the one found in the regular schools. It is truly humbling to spend the day, or week, with these kids. The smug complacency and occasional outrage we often exhibit when we hear about "problems in the city" as honest-to-god, taxpaying, *working* citizens can be pulverized by simply spending some one-on-one time with folks in that foreign environment.

Prior to this experience, I had never met anyone who had a radio monitor around their ankle. During the week in the alternative school I had a fourteen-year-old boy shyly admit that he had one on when he asked for a pass to the office to explain why he missed an appointment with his probation officer. When I asked him what he did to have such a device attached to his leg, he answered, "Stole a car."

I continue to scratch my head in disbelief when I think about the various stories I hear from these kids. The boy who persisted in sleeping in class told me that he couldn't get enough sleep the prior night "because of too much shooting in his neighborhood." Or the fifteen-year-old girl who told me that she needed to get a high school diploma so that she could get a better job and support her year-old baby.

The only time I hear shooting at night in my neighborhood is when one of the local rednecks is spotlighting a deer. And I *still* don't know anyone in my past circle of employed acquaintances that has a radio collar. Joe South had it completely right when he asked me to walk a mile in his shoes. It's really opened my eyes to the world around me.

It's really scary out there, but I never would have known about it—nor done anything about it—if I hadn't been suddenly unemployed.

# 50.

## SOMETIMES THEY FOOL YA

A wonderful character actress named Selma Diamond once remarked, during an episode of the TV series *Night Court* as actor Richard Moll passed by her, "Sometimes they fool ya when they walk upright." This statement comes to mind when I periodically run into another person who, although seeming capable of it, appears to be unemployed.

As I have discovered, as an unemployed person, I am capable of striking up a conversation with anyone. I once found myself seated next to a guy on a ski lift (hey, I'm unemployed—not a monk who took a vow of poverty—besides, I have discovered that most ski areas will offer free skiing to people who take part-time jobs there) and began a conversation with him. During the course of the ride up the mountain, made longer than usual due to several stops caused by inexperienced skiers falling off the chair at the top, I discovered several things.

We were both the same age, we both had approximately the same amount of mileage as skiers, we both had kids who were skiing that day, and—hang on now—he was *retired*. Whoa! Now *here* was a twist on handling "the question" that I hadn't thought about using to cover my tracks when someone asked.

Ernest Hemingway, another character actor who happened to be a damn-fine writer, once wrote that "one of the most important things that a writer can have is an infallible bullshit detector." Being unemployed for the length of time that I have been has possibly dulled my detector, because I haven't been surrounded by bull-shitters like I was when I was employed in the corporate world. When I tuned in to the guy next to me on the ski lift, I wasn't sure if he was telling me the truth, or if he had just played the "retired" card to put me off the track. I told him, quite truthfully, that I had been downsized and expected him to respond with some elaboration on his status. I really needed to know if my instincts were right.

The lift chair was headed, inexorably, toward the top of the mountain and the end of our conversation. I attempted to draw a little more information out of him before we had to unload and ski our separate ways. Anyone who skis knows that when you leave the lift, you never end up riding with the same stranger again—it's a kind of skiing karma thing. I used all of my conversational skills to draw him out and tell me from what he had retired, but was unsuccessful. Finally, in desperation, I mentioned that I wouldn't be able to get back to the ski area for a week due to travel commitments. He looked philosophical and said that he periodically had to travel during the winter due to consulting assignments.

*AH-HA!* He had used the "a little consulting" response and had shown his true colors! I could barely contain myself. I had discovered his secret. The guy was *unemployed*, just like me! He looked at me, grinning like the idiot I am, at times, and said, "Have a nice day" and skied off. I skied over to the top and watched him take off down the mountain to see if he was giving me the straight story about his skiing ability. He looked like a member of the U.S. Ski Team as he carved his way down the mountain.

Maybe he really *is* retired.

# 51.

## YES, MORE INTERVIEWS

A major part of the job for the suddenly unemployed always remains "finding" a job. Despite news to the contrary, the classified section of the newspaper often yields a few leads to follow—especially when your spouse or significant other (or, God forbid, your *parents*) says, "You know, we *really* need you to find *something.*"

*Something* is not necessarily (1) what you are qualified for, (2) what you really want to do with your life, or (3) what you can make a living wage with. Armed with these criteria, you begin scanning the classifieds anew and select opportunities that interest you. Occasionally, you find a nugget among the rubble and create a strategy for landing an interview.

I found a position in the newspaper that fairly leapt off the page as I read it. It was an advertising job with a publishing firm that I had previously approached. Never mind that they already had my resume, and that I had been assured by the publisher that "they would get back to me if something came up." I was going to wow these folks with my abilities and get that interview no matter what.

As you travel the path of the unemployed, you become smarter about some things and dumber about others. I was dumber than a stump for thinking that they would remember me from my previous foray into their offices. I was smarter for my experiences in the interview arena and my observations of company structure and hierarchy. Forget what I said about the Internet, it becomes critical to your success to learn every damn thing you can about some place that may possibly hire you.

I went to the publisher's website and read everything I could find about the company. I especially searched for listings of personnel and staff assignments. When I found out that the VP of advertising was a woman, all of the account executives had female names, and that all of the magazine titles seemed to be fully staffed, I knew I was probably going to end up being a "sacrifice interview."

I don't think that the term "sacrifice interview" appears in any self-help book that I have ever seen, so I'll claim the term as original with my experience. When you submit to a sacrifice interview, you are going in with the knowledge that the person or organization is going to suffer through thirty minutes with you so that they appear *fair* to all qualified applicants. I'm not sexist, but I am a guy who knows that appearing in the ladies room is going to have a fairly specific outcome. The same goes for ladies who are faced with a similar scenario. Only the strong survive.

Upon inquiry, it seemed that they "couldn't seem to find my earlier resume, and would I mind sending another copy." Again, it would have been easier upon my psyche to simply have faxed or e-mailed it to them, but I put on a nice tie and hand-delivered it. Contrary to popular opinion, particularly in light of numerous online resume posting services, I still believe that a personal appearance enhances your chances of being seen in the interview room —even if you are going as a "sacrifice."

Accordingly, I was granted an interview (probably based upon the fact that I was male and could fog a mirror with my breath) for the following week. Appearing on time, I was asked to spend twenty minutes scribbling upon an employment application that reiterated everything they already had on two previous resumes. Following that obligatory indignity, I was greeted by the VP of advertising and ushered into a conference room where, incredibly, I was asked to take a psychological aptitude test. Nobody ever said that getting turned down for a job was gonna be easy.

Following the preliminaries, I finally had an opportunity to display my interview prowess with the lady. And as I sat across from her and listened to the description cf the job, an idle thought crossed my mind. When you see television programs on sharks, have you ever noticed that they are never identified by sex? I suppose that the only way you can tell boy sharks from girl sharks is by gaffing one and dragging it on board the boat. Anyway, just listening to this prospective employer made me wonder what kind of shark was eyeing me up. She certainly wasn't a great white, but was well beyond the sand shark level; she probably weighed in as a tiger. Needless to say, after the perfunctory dialogue, I was offered the door, told that they would be making their decision in the near future, and would be notified of their decision. As a sacrifice interview, I had few illusions about what it would be.

Incidentally, this is an opportunity to discuss letters of rejection, an area in which I am an expert. It doesn't take a great amount of experience in the unemployment arena to gain a level of expertise in letters of rejection—just start taking interviews. One of the first clues to a letter of rejection is the appearance of an envelope with the company logo/return address on it. If you receive one of these envelopes, it contains a letter of rejection. And upon opening it, if the first word in the opening paragraph is "although," you may consider yourself officially rejected. Generally, the initial word is followed by "your credentials are impressive." The only variations to this theme are attempts by the sender to deviate from tradition by shuffling the announcement of bad news or by using some creativity in delivering the unwanted announcement. One of the ones that made my list of memorable rejections was the sentence, "I selected an applicant with a more *customized* background."

I really liked that one. It made me feel like an Escort in a parking lot full of street rods.

# 52.

## FIVE JOBS I, AND YOU, ARE QUALIFIED TO DO

After a period of unemployment, or even underemployment, you lift the veil and start to do some serious self-evaluation. You *know* what you have on your resume, but no one seems to be riveted by your technological, educational, or experiential prowess. After sufficient time and rejection, you begin to question your ability to gain a foothold in the working world where you *should* be. You need to take a hard look at your experience and abilities and do a serious self-assessment.

I have identified five jobs that I haven't held but *I know* I am qualified to do.

*TALK SHOW HOST*

After a period of unemployment, you have watched sufficient television to know that after infomercials, talk shows rule airwaves that would otherwise be vacant. You don't have to be famous (but it helps), good looking (but it helps), or even have extensive educational credentials. You *do* have to be reasonably articulate, willing to put up with some truly outrageous behavior, and be willing to be canceled at a moment's notice. I qualify.

*CONVENIENCE STORE CLERK*

As an unemployed person, you have the opportunity during the day to run down to the local convenience store for a newspaper to check the classifieds. You *know* that you don't have to be famous, good looking, or even have a high school diploma to do this job. You *do* have to be able to pass a police background check and a drug test. I qualify.

*PRESIDENT OF THE UNITED STATES*

As strange as it seems, because I was born in America, I have reached the obligatory age requirement, and don't have any felony convictions, I qualify.

*RAP ARTIST*

Requires no education, police background check, or drug test. Does require the ability to rhyme and hold a microphone. Again, I qualify.

*BARTENDER*

Does not require any extensive education, but does require the ability to mix drinks, tell jokes, and listen to an endless collection of bores giving you their opinion (remember, I *did* work for a large corporation). Once again, I qualify.

# 53.

## THINNING THE HERD

It's one thing to be unemployed as a twentysomething, or even a thirtysomething, person. It's quite another to be forty- or fiftysomething and in need of employment. In your twenties and thirties you have the comfort of knowing that the world is ahead of you and that someone will always take you aboard, because you're young, ambitious, and will probably be willing to work for less money. As an older person, likely having greater financial obligations, you simply can't afford to take a flyer on an entry-level position that may develop into something more.

As a younger (and single) man, I found it easier to be impulsive about my work habits and location. In 1975 I was fed up with what I was doing and where I was living and simply loaded all of my personal belongings in the back of a pickup truck and moved six hundred miles away. No job, no place to live, no attachments. I had the luxury of youthful self-determination. I quickly found an apartment, a job, and a new circle of friends. Of course, my parents were alarmed and concerned at my abrupt change of address and cautioned me about things like "career choices" and "being a member of a community," but it was the seventies, and I was young. My parents were healthy and well established in their lives. My siblings were doing what they wanted. Life was ahead of us all.

As time passed, I met the woman of my dreams, got married, and started a family. Pretty traditional, huh? We struggled financially, finally built a house, started buying cars with loans attached to them, and both worked on building rewarding careers. It was such an exhilarating experience that we seemed not to notice that the years were going by. And one day as I surveyed the stuff in the garage to see what could be stashed somewhere else so that we could get both cars inside, I had an epiphany. My life had changed; I was growing older, and there was no way that I could even get the stuff that I wanted to *throw away* into the back of a pickup truck!

I began to look around with a new sense of vision. As a twenty and thirtysomething, I never gave any thought to growing older and worrying about a pension or social security, or replacing the roof on the house we built (hey, we paid extra to get the thirty-year shingles!). As a fortysomething, I was seeing my parents growing older and suffering from ailments that they didn't seem to have before. My parents' friends were all growing older, too. Some of them were retiring, some were dying.

The year prior to being downsized by my corporate employer, my mother died. She died very suddenly of a heart attack, and I was thrown into the whirlwind of a family tragedy for the first time in my life. At the same time, my wife's father began suffering a series of debilitating illnesses, which resulted in his passing within months of my mother's death. And although we both had lost parents, my wife and I had the comfort of knowing that we were gainfully employed and could weather the storm, no matter what.

On that fateful day that I was cut from the corporate team, I didn't realize how important my lack of employment could be to other members of my extended family. My father, always a true rock in our family, showed me the importance of simply "being there" for others. He had retired (unemployed, but *with* the money) and was able to spend more time traveling with my mother and enjoying the golden years. When my father-in-law, Henry, became ill and eventually homebound, most of his friends and business associates seemed to, understandably, have commitments that precluded them from spending time with him—except for my dad. My father made a point of making the half-hour drive to Henry's home and taking him to lunch weekly. He was the only one of Henry's friends and associates that made that kind of an effort to comfort a dying man.

When I found myself in unemployment's grip, I found that I could easily make the time to clean gutters, pick up a car at the repair shop, paint a ceiling, stack firewood, go Christmas shopping, and pick up a prescription—all for someone else. Instead of dwelling upon my own problem, I could literally put it aside for a while and focus on the needs of another. It's a very liberating experience for the suddenly unemployed. And as time has passed during this period in my life, I have found some degree of enlightenment in being able to simply be there. As my father has grown older, and has suffered the debilitation accompanying Parkinson's disease, I have been able to be there. When my brother was diagnosed with a rapidly advancing form of cancer, the ten-hour drive to visit with him was a small inconvenience compared to the wonderful quality of time spent with him prior to his death.

As time passes and the herd thins out, it becomes more evident to me—the unemployed guy—that simply being there for your family and friends is more important than being there for an employer.

# 54.

## PEOPLE WHO ARE EMPLOYED IN JOBS IN WHICH I HAVE NO INTEREST BUT ARE INTERESTING NONETHELESS

I know this title is a mouthful, but I can't think of it in any other terms. It is always fascinating to me as to how some people end up in the jobs that they have, and seem to either like them or make the best of it. I imagine few of us look longingly at the grab handle on the back of a garbage truck and think, "Gee, there's a job I could really get into." Just looking at the guys doing that job tells you that it probably pays the bills, but as soon as something better comes along—like driving the truck—they're history.

My wife hates bugs. Well, perhaps hate is too strong a word, she really doesn't like certain bugs like fleas and ticks. And since we have dogs, we have fleas and ticks entering the house astride the hounds. Fleas don't bother me, because they don't bite me, but ticks seem to find me tasty. As a result, we have an exterminator treat the house on a regular basis. The exterminator has one of those jobs in which I have no interest. But when you are unemployed, you have the golden opportunity to spend some time with the "bug man."

Our bug man, Jack (not his real name), takes his job very seriously. He has, on occasion, provided me with in-depth discourse on the chemical composition of the poisons he spreads about our house. I politely listen to descriptions of "micro-encapsulation" of various industrial venoms specifically designed to eliminate critters with six and eight legs, but not mammals standing on two or four. Jack discusses the problems he encounters with the gravity of a corporate vice-president. I don't know what his employers pay him, but they would be amazed by his presentation of the industry he represents.

Another job that doesn't appeal to me, but I have a great respect for, is the one that has a member of the Salvation Army standing next to the red tripod and bucket in front of department stores across America from the day after Thanksgiving until Christmas. I think that what they do is wonderful, but don't they get sick of ringing that bell nonstop for a month? And if there are members of the Salvation Army in front of all those department stores in America for a month, how many people are employed at this task? More perplexing to me is what they do the *other* eleven months out of the year.

In a shopping mall nearby there is a nice lady who runs a candy kiosk near the cinema complex. Given the price of snacks inside the theater, she does a sensational business, and since we unemployed types are always looking for a way to save money, I have developed a passing acquaintanceship with her. The thing that amazes me about her business is the fact that she is *always* there. If we go to the movies on a Friday, she is there. If we go on Sunday, she is there. If we go to a "twilight feature" on a Wednesday, there she is. She never seems to leave the kiosk. I wonder why you can't get this kind of employee devotion in American corporate culture?

There is a convenience store in the small town nearest my home that, although most of the work force changes regularly, has a few regulars that always seem to be in evidence. One of the employees, Dot (her real name), always seems to be in the store in some capacity. The more you shop for milk, eggs, bread and lunchmeat, the better you get to know those who work in the store. Once, when I arrived on my motorcycle to pick up a few staples, Dot informed me that she used to have a motorcycle and had ridden across the Mojave Desert on it. Having established that bond, Dot and I became conversant on a variety of subjects, particularly the local doings that require police attention. She is my source for much of the neighborhood gossip. Once, for a period of a few weeks, she disappeared. When I inquired as to her whereabouts, I was informed that "she quit but she's comin' back next week." And she did. I guess that when you don't have paid vacation or benefits, you need to empower yourself and become unemployed just to get time off.

# 55.

# A MATTER OF PERCEPTION

In our household we receive many, many offers in the mail. Offers from credit card companies inviting us to "use these checks" to solve our financial woes. Offers from life insurance companies that, for some reason, call themselves "life *assurance* companies." (Why on earth would I pay money to have my life *assured*? As long as I blink when someone touches my eyeball, I'm assured that I'm alive for free.) Offers for free water testing. Offers for replacement windows with a chance to win a free set of windows just for responding. The list goes on, and on, and on.

Years ago we received an invitation to "visit" a place called "Outdoor World" and receive a free gift for just listening to the pitch. My wife decided that we should go to get the free gas grill that was promised. We went, sat through an incredibly tedious and high pressure sales pitch for a *seven thousand dollar* "master" membership in a campground, and came away with a hibachi powered by one of those propane cylinders that you use to thaw frozen pipes.

Recently, an offer came in the mail for us to "make an appointment" to visit a membership buying "club" that came with an automobile ignition key to a new Cadillac and a guarantee that we would win two of five prizes listed on the brochure. When you're unemployed for a considerable time, these things gain in significance, particularly when hope becomes a major factor in your personal business plan. The prizes included a high-end personal computer, a large flat-screen television, $500 in cash, a ladies tennis bracelet (a $49 value!), and a three-day vacation getaway ($50 refundable deposit required and no airfare included). Somehow, the prospect of that Caddy to replace the aging Isuzu and that PC and flat-screen TV seemed too much to pass up.

After the third call from a member of the public relations department insisting that we schedule an appointment to visit the showroom, I agreed to appear and find out what opportunities awaited. Incredibly, my wife agreed to accompany me on this venture. Actually, she had to, since attendance by both husband and wife were required to qualify for the prizes. We agreed to appear at 3:15 on a Saturday afternoon at a city nearly forty-five minutes from our home. Like Robert Duvall in *Apocalypse Now*, I smelled victory.

Arriving at the membership showroom, which was located, oddly, in the middle of an industrial park, we were given adhesive name tags, upon which we wrote our names and were invited by a member of the public relations staff (who also had one of those adhesive name tags) to sit down for a brief interrogation, er, introduction. And after deftly deflecting questions about where we were employed, what we thought our joint incomes were, and what we thought we would be making in major home purchases for the next ten years, we were moved to a small room to watch a videotape. The room was warm, the videotape was basically an infomercial, which repetitively extolled the virtues of membership in the discount club, and I began to doze off. After the videotape ended, the real show began with the appearance of the sales manager (funny, he didn't refer to himself as a member of the public relations staff once during his presentation).

In the world of sales, this guy was the "closer." He repeated everything that was pounded into us by the videotape, and then took us out to show us some of the discount catalogs from which we could save "twenty, forty, up to sixty percent under retail" for products from major manufacturers. At one point, he referred to some fine china as part of the "debit" collection. And as I pondered what debits had to do with dinnerware, I looked at the catalog page and realized that he was pronouncing "debut" in a manner heretofore unknown to me. As he scratched himself and looked around the small crowd of husbands and wives surrounding him, he delivered the words we all were waiting for: "And, for only $3,500 for the first three years, and $1,000 per year for the next three, you can have access to prices that only retail-store buyers know about." Well, it was cheaper than that darn campground.

My wife and I kindly declined, amidst protestations that this was the only opportunity that we would be allowed for membership in the club, and asked if we could try the key in the Cadillac and pick up our prizes. It's funny, but I hadn't noticed any gleaming example of Detroit's finest sitting anywhere around the showroom, and there was a reason. The key was to be inserted into a fake ignition switch mounted in a piece of Masonite near the door of the showroom. It didn't fit. Then a member of the "public relations staff" handed us a small box with a ladies tennis bracelet (with genuine Austrian crystals set in the band) and a colorful flyer from "Vacation Getaways" for us to peruse at our leisure somewhere outside of the building.

As we sat in the car, numb from mental exhaustion, my dear, sweet wife said, "I feel like I was just in hell." I nodded knowingly, and said, "Yes, I know what you mean; I can't *imagine* doing that for a living!" She looked at me strangely and said, "No, I meant that hell must be like having to sit through one of those presentations over, and over again."

See, it really *is* a matter of perception.

# 56.

## GOING TO THE HEAD OF THE CLASS

I recently received an invitation to attend a high school class reunion. This, in itself, is not normally a daunting proposition provided you still have most of your hair and haven't gained more than thirty pounds since you graduated. Fortunately, I qualify in both respects, although the hair is no longer dark brown. What is chilling about this adventure is just exactly what the hell I'm going to say about myself to people I haven't seen in thirty-five years.

Actually, I didn't graduate with this class, although I spent most of my formative years with many of them. This class donned their mortarboards without me, because I was graduating from a high school five hundred miles away. For some reason, probably a mid-life crisis, my father sold his insurance business and took a job as the manager of a summer camp. This meant that I was given the opportunity to leave all of my lifetime friends at the end of tenth grade and move to Michigan. To add insult to autonomy, my parents (actually, my mother) decided that I needed to go to PRIVATE SCHOOL to further my education.

The private school that they selected was not only in Michigan, it was a private school run by Christian Scientists in *upper* Michigan. Not only was I denied the use of my snazzy 1956 Ford, I was denied the companionship and solace of my family—the only people I even *knew* in that mosquito-infested haven of America's rust belt. Needless to say, I was miserable even though my mother had the pleasure of telling *her* new friends that "Ricky (jeez, she called me that my entire life) is going to private school."

The school was located at the edge of Lake Michigan and was populated by a combination of kids from Christian Scientist families, and rich kids who had been thrown out of school in the suburbs of Detroit. Obviously, I was drawn to the juvenile delinquents—my only consolation during the period of my incarceration at a private institution of learning. On the plus side was the fact that the curriculum was, to say the least, not rigorous, and I managed to pass geometry (after failing Algebra I and Algebra II previously). When I'd had enough of early-morning religious training and wearing uniforms (yes, uniforms—navy blue blazers, white shirts, gray slacks, and the school tie), I called my dad and offered an ultimatum: "You can come and pick me up, or meet me at the bus station, because I'm coming home."

He picked me up the next day, and I was enrolled in the local high school in Michigan where I knew virtually no one and graduated at the end of the year. I was, however, voted "most sophisticated" by the senior class, and when I asked a classmate why I was so honored, he replied, "Uh, 'cause they didn't have a category for stuck up." Gee, what wonders that did for my fragile ego (I was shy and didn't really communicate with my peers, and I thought most of them were a subspecies of the human race, too).

I graduated and never went back. I'm probably not even on the "Where Are They Now?" page.

Back to the present and my present problem; what to say when someone asks "the question." Do I make up some sort of carefully crafted response that says something, and at the same time, nothing? Like, "I'm doing some consulting." Or do I bare my soul and tell them that I'm unemployed, and that I've been unemployed for a long time, and do they know anyone who's hiring? *That* should send them back to the buffet in a hurry.

Fortunately, I have enough lead time on this event that I can prepare myself for the litany of questions that accompany a thirty-five-year absence. This particular class has a website for the reunion, which is filled with information about the event, a "Where Are They Now?" page and, curiously, a "Gone but Not Forgotten" page. When I clicked on the "Where Are They Now" button, I reviewed the names and noticed only one that I could identify regarding whereabouts (he works in a foreign car parts store where I purchase things for the aging Isuzu). It was when I clicked on the "Gone but Not Forgotten" button that I was really appalled. There were nearly thirty former classmates who had—and there's no euphemistic way to approach it—died.

The looking glass of remembrance is most unkind when you think about how much time has passed and how much the world, and your peers, have changed. I can accept bald, fat, arthritic, famous, boring (actually, the boring people were usually boring in high school, too), successful, much-married and divorced, broke, pitiful, born-again, overbearing (ditto on the high school thing), shallow, self-indulgent, much-educated, and genuinely nice. I just have a hard time accepting dead. When we were in high school, we were immortal, we were, well, gods. The whole world was before us, and we were the generation that was going to change it. How on earth could thirty of us have died in so short a time? Somehow, worrying about my employment problem didn't seem quite so momentous anymore.

So I'll send my money in to the class treasurer, try to lose a few pounds, get a killer haircut, and maybe some new clothes, put my lovely wife in the nicest car we own (she doesn't have to worry, she went to a different school, and she's got a career), and go to the reunion.

# 57.

## YOU'RE NEVER TOO OLD

Once, some time ago, a news report appeared regarding "America's Oldest Teenager" and the lawsuit that had been filed against him. It seems that the late Dick Clark, at the age of seventy-four, was being sued by an individual who said that he was the victim of age discrimination. It seems that the former host of American Bandstand rejected the hiring of the gentleman in question because he was too old. Gee, the guy was *only* seventy-six years old. That news story caused my white, thinning hair to bristle at the number of times I think I was rejected in job interviews for the same reason.

Being prematurely gray, or, in my case, prematurely white, isn't something that I dwell upon—except in a job interview. I generally get the sense that the interviewer is looking at me and thinking, "Why is this old guy even interviewing?" I have, on numerous occasions, volunteered my age (knowing that they can't ask that question) to counteract the sense that I am being viewed as too old for whatever I am interviewing. The response is generally a look of bemused satisfaction, or pity, with an occasional slightly arched eyebrow. I have considered taking my birth certificate with me just to prove my lack of longevity on this mortal coil.

You are never too old to do a job well. You can be too dumb, or too inflexible, or too ill, or too inexperienced, but you can never be too old—unless you believe you are. I have friends who passed the seventy mark who are relentless workers and activists. My attorney, who was a fraternity brother of my father, has passed the age of eighty and still goes to the office every day. He was the chief litigator for a large law firm until they made him retire at the mandatory age. The day after he "retired" he hung a shingle on a new office and continued business as usual. He also took a number of his clients with him on his new venture. I am always in awe of this man; a warhorse in the truest sense of the word.

Another friend, also retired—from the CIA (well, I think it's the CIA—he's real cagey about what he did for the government) and an avid skier, walks several miles every day in the warm months and works as a ski instructor every day when the snow is on the mountain. He's seventy-four and was voted one of the top one hundred ski instructors in America several years ago by *Ski* magazine. Amazingly, he didn't take up skiing until he was forty-three.

Yet another friend, retired from the educational arena, promptly took up real estate after he checked out of high school administration. He collects vintage sports cars, works all seven days of many weeks during the prime real estate season, and manages a trip to Europe periodically. He is seventy-eight and considers a normal bike ride (he has, at least, five bicycles in his garage) about fifteen miles. Depending on the weather, these bike rides are thrice weekly.

I wonder if Dick Clark would have considered any of these gentlemen too old to work for him?

# 58.

## YOU KNOW YOU'RE A CANDIDATE FOR DOWNSIZING WHEN ...

I don't really know what the rationale for downsizing really is. I think it's a secret (kinda like Colonel Sanders's recipe—hey! another whitehair who wouldn't quit working!!!) that corporations keep locked in the company safe. I do know that a lot of men (take note) in their late fifties (again take note) seem to have their jobs "eliminated" and are given the opportunity to find positions elsewhere in the company—or be let go (downsized). This occurs usually during times of economic distress and when hiring freezes are in place. Gosh, what's a fella to do when his position has been eliminated and the company isn't hiring ...

You know that you're currently a candidate for downsizing if any of the following apply:

- Other employees refer to you as "one of the grayhairs."
- You know who Gabby Hayes was.
- You remember when the Vietnam War started.

- Your first car would now qualify for antique license tags.
- Your first house cost less than your new car.
- You still have a collection of LPs (younger collectors call them "vinyl").
- You still have a collection of cassette tapes—and listen to them.
- You have a madras shirt that you just can't bear to part with.

# 59.

## GHOULS

Over the years I have managed to find at least two jobs by being a ghoul. That's not to say that I crept into a cemetery and dug someone up, but I did manage to benefit from the demise of a predecessor. At one point, while trying to make a living as a freelance writer of equestrian-related topics, I ran across an obituary for an editor of a national horse racing trade journal. The gentleman who had crossed the finish line in life's great race had been an editor at that particular magazine for a number of years. Upon learning of his passing, I wasted no time in gathering my clips and making an appointment with the publisher, who hired me on the spot—for, as I learned later, considerably less money than he had been paying the former editor.

The editor's job, which paid $275 a week, required fifty to sixty hours of my time in that seven-day span, and included not only editing, but rewrite, photo selection, ad preparation, layout, and travel to racetracks throughout the northeastern United States. It was, to say the least, a learning experience.

Another position that I managed to acquire by being a ghoul was with the corporation that eventually downsized me. Again, I learned of the passing of a technical editor in the publications department of the company through a friend. And, again, I hurried to make an appointment with the manager of the department. Admittedly, I had very few credentials as a technical writer but found that the manager was a true automotive junkie and a talker of prodigious duration. After suffering through an incredibly tedious monologue regarding the various cars that this gentleman had owned, he told me that "they would let me know" in a week what their decision would be. This time I was a little smarter about salary negotiation and, when the call came, I was ready.

"Rick, I talked to the old man (*his* boss and, as I learned, the guy who made all of the decisions), and we'd like to have you on board."

"That's great," I replied.

"We're going to start you at $18,000 per year," he said.

At this point I was somewhat dumbfounded, since our previous discussion had centered around a much higher figure. Not knowing what to say, I allowed a significant amount of time to pass in the conversation, which was the smartest move I could have made.

"Well, what do you think?" he said.

"Gee, I'm going to have to think about that," I said. "I'll have to let you know."

That little pause in the conversation was worth an additional $5,000 per year, and the knowledge that most companies will try to buy you for the least amount of money. It also made me realize that I had managed to work myself into a company that was a leader in the electronics industry, with literally no knowledge of the business at hand.

Scary, isn't it?

# 60.

## WHAT I *HAVE* LEARNED

Having your career "feet" kicked out from under you by loss of a job is a shattering experience. Even if you can see it coming, the actual act is always a surprise. To go from the relative security of a steady job to the panic of sudden unemployment is humbling. The outrage of being denied *your* position by another (be it an individual or corporate committee) is something that no one but the suddenly unemployed can appreciate. If there is anything that I wish that I could bring to the awareness of people who are responsible for ending the dreams of others, it would be that sense of outrage and denial. If I could legislate anything for the corporate world, I would require that anyone in charge of firing (or downsizing) people be a victim of that peculiar situation as part of their job description. Our employment climate has shifted from that of caring what the organization needs to produce something worthwhile, to one of pragmatism for the bottom line. Milton S. Hershey, creator of the candy bar and the empire that bears his name, saw his company through the Great Depression in the 1930s without firing any employees in the name of business. Granted, his employees had to make some concessions in order to maintain their positions, but none were let go in order to improve the company's bottom line. Needless to say, Mr. Hershey never would have said, "It's nothing personal, it's just business."

With the passage of time, the sense of outrage diminishes and the need for affirmation increases. And as you pass through a series of near misses in the quest for employment—affirmation—the banked fires of outrage periodically are blown back into flames. I have learned that keeping your sense of humor is the best way of damping those fires. Your sense of humor is a shield, a talisman for maintaining your perspective in a time of uncertainty and diminished self-esteem. If you lose your sense of humor in the climate of unemployment, you give in to the injustice that has been done to you.

During the period of time that I have been suddenly unemployed I have lost my brother, my father, and my mother-in-law; all of them are people who have had a significant impact upon my life. My brother, no matter how distressed his life may have been, could always make me laugh at myself with his often raffish sense of humor. My father, always the one who appeared distinguished and taciturn, had a dry wit and a bemused vision of this crazy world. And my mother-in-law had seemingly no sense of humor, which made her even funnier to me. I suffered their loss greatly and still miss them very much. The one thing they all had in common was their belief in me.

Through it all, one person has persevered and believed in me unfailingly, my wife, Tris. Without her, I would never have weathered this emotional storm. I would, quite literally, have perished beneath the waves of despair, which periodically engulfed me. Her belief that I *could* succeed is what has always allowed me to endure this passage in life and to permit my sense of humor and self-esteem to carry me forward. She has been both my rock and my lodestone. She has provided direction and constructive criticism, while remaining the most desirable woman I know. I am, indeed, blessed by her existence.

My children, Emily and Aaron, have also allowed me to grow in ways that I could not have anticipated. Although they are both young and still finding their respective paths in life, they have both paused on the roadway to allow the old man to catch up and share their joy. They both give me great pride and often provide me with insights into the state of the world in their eyes—a vision that is often denied people of my age.

To those who are carrying the burden of seeking new paths in life, whether it be caused by forces beyond their control, or simply because choosing a new route seems, well, *right*, I applaud your enterprising spirit. It's not a cold, cruel world out there if you arm yourself with what really matters most—family, good friends, and good advice. Seek all unceasingly, and do not allow yourself to be dissuaded by negative spirits and those who would tell you that you *can't* do something that you feel is right for *you*. I am reminded of an instance when my father, who also went through a period of mid-life "adjustment," assumed a task for an employer for which I questioned his skills. When I said, "Do you know anything about that?" he replied, "No, but *they* don't know that."

Always reply in the affirmative when someone asks you to do something. And if the task exceeds your abilities, or expectations, ask someone you trust for help. Only through initiative and self-esteem can you succeed in a world that has turned you out on your own. Use your sense of humor and your sense of wonder to push yourself forward. And if you still can't find an appropriate place for yourself in the social order of the "working world" you can always write a book.

THE END

# ACKNOWLEDGMENTS

Books are created not only by the author but by the contributions of others in the developmental process. I would like to thank my mother for instilling the love of reading in me and wish that she could have read this one. I'd also like to thank Michael and Rosalie Pakenham for their early encouragement in this book, Lawrence Knorr for allowing it to become a reality, and Janice Rhayem for a skillful edit of it. My greatest thanks go to the person who has been my greatest inspiration, my best friend, constant companion, love of my life, and wife, Tris.

www.ingramcontent.com/pod-product-compliance
Lightning Source LLC
Chambersburg PA
CBHW050508210326
41521CB00011B/2379